food from
green places

food from Green Places

vegetarian recipes from garden & countryside

ROSAMOND RICHARDSON

photographs by Robin Matthews

Abbeville Press Publishers
New York London Paris

contents

Introduction

My life was rich: I took a swarm of bees

And found a crumpled snake skin on the road,

All in one day, and was increased by these.

I have not understood humanity.

But those plain things, that gospel of each year,

Made me the scholar of simplicity.

The Land, Vita Sackville-West, 1926

The concept of a "rural idyll" is deeply ingrained in the human psyche: The Garden of Eden is mankind's original myth. The powerful longing for some connection with the countryside, with things natural, is a desire for peace, tranquillity, and security away from the insanities of urban life. People find this in their own ways: If they are not able to live in the country, they may find a personal oasis through tending their own garden, of whatever size, to produce their own food from green places.

Here the echoes of a rural past still ring clear. For centuries our predecessors have harvested their garden produce through the turning seasons of the year. They have gathered food from field and forest, tended their fruit trees and bushes, worked on the vegetable plot, and planted herb gardens for medicinal as well as culinary use. The more dedicated have kept bees, and produced their own honey for themselves and their neighbors. Many have had chickens scratching around to produce farm fresh eggs, and the more courageous naturalists have foraged for mushrooms in spring and fall. Country folk have made wines, cordials, and herbal teas for generations, using all manner of basic materials: Their skill was in making use of everything that grew around them, as well as what they cultivated, and in knowing their various properties and qualities.

It is a long heritage, starting in Europe with the monastic gardens of the Middle Ages, but basically stretching back to the ancient history of the Far East, Egypt, the Middle East, and ancient Greece and Rome. The botanical names of fruits, flowers, herbs, and vegetables reflect their far-flung origins and cultures, and their history is full of fascinating stories. The gardens of the East are now but legend, but we can still find traces of the earliest Western infirmary gardens planted by medieval monks. From there it is a rich trail through sixteenth-century formal gardens to the great age of the stately home in the eighteenth and early nineteenth centuries, until we reach the softer influence of English garden designers Gertrude Jekyll and William Robinson, as they returned to the more natural look of the cottage garden. Yet, whatever the scale of

the garden and however humble or elegant its design, the underlying purpose has always been twofold: The harvesting of home-grown produce and the joy of living with plants in the garden.

The garden harvest tells us much about economic history at any given moment in time. Food is a social barometer; it is closely connected with the fluctuations of civilization. It is also about self-sufficiency, about making use of everything that we can grow, and of the plants in the wild. In addition, the many myths attached to these plants have been woven into a rich tapestry of folklore over the centuries, which is just as alive today as it ever was. Delving into old recipe books takes us directly into the insights of our forebears, and many an old manuscript provides amusing comments or instructions which capture the feeling of a particular time. They describe old country traditions, many of which are still extant today in parts of rural Europe.

The style of cooking in *Food From Green Places* owes much to this rural heritage. Some of it is traditional English country cooking, some of it owes something to the more eclectic styles of modern living. But the majority of recipes have an intrinsically peasant quality to them—simplicity and honesty being the keynotes. The concession to healthy eating is evident: Whereas in the past people ate a diet rich in animal fats, the recipes in this book tend to favor vegetable margarines over butter, and make plentiful use of olive and sunflower oils. The use of sugar is kept low, and *crème fraîche* and plain yogurt replace light and heavy cream. Where you are using much of your own organic produce, it is logical to use farm fresh eggs and foods which have minimum processing, such as raw sugar and wholewheat or unbleached flours, or a balance of both. The food has an integrity; it is natural and wholesome, healthy and clean. Food from green places is good food. It is also a personal response to the mysterious subtlety and awesome beauty of the seasonal cycle.

abundant *Orchards*

An apple I took of a tree

God had it forbidden me

Wherefore I should damned be

14th century ms, *Anon*

According to legend, Mesopotamia's Garden of Eden was full of fruit trees, and Middle Eastern orchards were also pleasure gardens. The word "orchard" means enclosed garden, and would usually shelter apple, pear, and plum trees. The Song of Songs sings, "As the apple tree among the trees of the orchard, so is my beloved among the young men."

In medieval Europe, fruit was used more for making drinks than for eating, and cider was the most common drink in England in the Middle Ages. Desserts, heavily sweetened and spiced, appear in manuscript recipes, and preserves were commonplace in all households, providing variety during the lean winter months. Cottagers and small farmers invariably had one or two fruit trees for their own use, enabling them to stock the larder. Their cottage gardens provided means of self-sufficiency: A vegetable patch, chickens, perhaps a pig, a beehive or two, and at the very least an apple tree. For the richer, as part of their larger estates, a formal orchard might be enclosed within the kitchen garden or set just outside its vine-clad walls.

Legendary from the earliest times, the apple became highly symbolic in biblical and mythological terms, being a sign of fertility and good luck. Apples probably came to England with the Romans, before which time the crab apple was widely used in drinks, vinegars, and sour cooking cider. The pear became a symbol of delight, and Edward I commanded "peares" to be planted in his garden at Westminster: The kings of England were the principal fruit growers in their land. The wild pear, native to England, was popular in preserves, jams, and desserts, and perry was a popular drink among country folk. The quince was the next favorite, used for marmalade, jelly and preserves. According to archive records, the king's gardener at the Palace of Westminster bought a lot of quince, pear, and apple trees in 1292, the quinces costing 41 shillings per 100, the same price as a peach tree but vastly more expensive than a cherry tree, which in those days fetched about 1s 6d (about 20 cents) per 100.

Peaches feature in medieval literature from the thirteenth century onward, usually classed as exotic fruit,

and were a royal favorite. *The Chronicle of Roger of Wendover*, 1210, tells us that King John hastened his own death by indulging in "a surfeit of peaches and ale." The fruit of the curious medlar, that Chaucer called a "homely tree," was made into preserves by many, and the gardener at Westminster Abbey was ordered to supply the community with *"apples, cherries in season, plums, big pears, nuts, and mepsilia [medlars] if he has them in his garden."* The fruit was stored in straw for a month, from October to November, when it was eaten in its softened state, either raw or puréed with honey.

Not everyone bothered to cultivate plums in those days, since wild plums were plentiful: John Gerard's *Herbal* of 1597 refers to cultivars as "manured," and in his day the gardens at Westminster Abbey won acclaim for the sweetness of their cultivated plums. Damsons, bullace, and sloes were gathered from country lanes in the fall as part of the annual wild harvest. Mulberries, eaten ripe from the tree, were also deemed useful as a food dye, and their juice, which makes an invigorating drink in its own right, was added both to wine and to plum "pottage."

Raspberries were picked wild rather than cultivated: They grew prolifically alongside elderberries, blackberries, and bilberries in English lanes and hedgerows. Strawberries, on the other hand, were imported as early as the thirteenth century, and by the fifteenth century they had become fashionable, often sold by the street sellers of London. The earliest record of cultivated gooseberries, which even though native to Britain were rarely used in the Middle Ages, is dated 1275, in the reign of Edward I. Interestingly enough, they featured only in savory dishes. Cherries, eaten "wine-red," were widely cultivated and highly valued: King Henry VIII's fruiterer established cherry orchards at Newington in Kent, an area still famous for its fruit.

Over the following centuries, as the art of gardening developed, orchards and kitchen gardens evolved from purely practical considerations into the beginnings of an art form: The legacy of the medieval arbor becomes the inspiration for a tunnel of fruit trees trained over an iron frame, the traditional "potager" evolves from monastic plots, and the beauty of espaliered fruit trees graces many a sunny wall in many a land.

Traditional APPLE TART

There are endless versions of apple pies, tarts, and flans. Gervase Markham's *The English Housewife* of 1683 gives a traditional English recipe:

TO MAKE APPLE TART: Take apples and peel them, and slice them thin from the core into a pan with white wine, good store of sugar, cinnamon and rose water, and so boil all till it be thick. Then cool it and strain it, and beat it very well together with a spoon, and then put it into your crust and bake it. It carrieth the color red.

Apples

According to Genesis, the apple was the first fruit of the world's creation. Cooks through the ages have invented countless ways of using them, and here are some recipes which include a number of traditional old English ideas, adapted to modern tastes and techniques. Many have the flavor of peasant cuisine—English country cooking at its most genuine and natural.

Autumnal Apple Crisp

These fragrantly spiced apples have a unique freshness and crunchy texture, and the crisp topping of this wonderful dessert is mouthwatering. You can use pears in place of apples, as both fruits make a memorable and original dessert.

SERVES 6

4 cups day-old bread crumbs

ground nutmeg and apple pie spice, for dusting

1½ lb baking apples, peeled and cored

sugar to taste

1 teaspoon apple pie spice

¼ cup candied lemon peel, chopped

a little butter or margarine

Grease an 8-inch pie dish and cover thickly with 1 cup of bread crumbs. Dust with a sprinkling of nutmeg and apple pie spice.

Coarsely grate the apples and mix with ½ cup of the bread crumbs, sugar to taste, the 1 teaspoon apple pie spice, and the candied peel. Pile into the prepared dish. Cover the top thickly with the last of the bread crumbs and dot with butter or margarine. Bake in a preheated oven at 375°F for 30 minutes, until the crust is crisp and brown. It is delicious hot or warm.

An old recipe book recommends serving this with hot chocolate sauce. My preference would be for thick plain yogurt or perhaps custard sauce (see *Crème Anglaise* on page 153), although I have memories of my mother grating chocolate over a hot dish of grated, baked apples, and it was exquisite.

Nursery APPLES

There is an old English recipe that instructs the cook to core apples and fill the holes with brown sugar. They are then packed into a dish, water added to halfway up the fruit, and baked until the apples are fluffy and the sugar has boiled to toffee.

French Apple Tart
In the past, country people brought apples and medlars to church on All Saints Day as an offering to the souls of the departed, and such traditions still survive in parts of France today. The French have a great tradition of apple cookery, and make an apple tart that takes some beating for all its simplicity.

SERVES 6–8

1 recipe quantity Sweet Crust Dough (see page 150)

4–5 medium apples

1 tablespoon lemon juice

2 large egg yolks

2–2½ tablespoons vanilla sugar

1 cup heavy cream

Roll out the dough and use to line a greased 10-inch tart pan. Bake blind (see page 152) in a preheated oven at 400°F for 15 minutes. Cool a little on a wire rack.

Peel, core, and slice the apples, sprinkling them as you do so with lemon juice to prevent discoloration. Beat together the egg yolks with the vanilla sugar until thick and pale, then beat in the cream.

Arrange the apple slices in a circular pattern over the cooked pastry shell, pointed ends toward the center. Pour over the cream mixture and bake in the oven at 375°F for 30–35 minutes, until the cream is nearly set firm but still slightly runny in the center. Let cool slightly. Serve warm.

Apple Turnovers
Simply wonderful: Crisp golden puff pastry, encased around an aromatic apple sauce; these turnovers melt in the mouth.

MAKES 8

6 Macoun, Northern Spy, or other crisp, tart apples, peeled, cored, and chopped

sugar to taste

a pinch of ground cinnamon

1 tablespoon chopped candied orange peel

2 teaspoons rosewater

1 teaspoon dill seeds (optional)

½ lb store-bought puff pastry, rolled out very thinly

sunflower oil, for frying

sugar, for sprinkling

Cook the chopped apples with a little water until you have a thick, smooth purée. Sweeten to taste with a little sugar and add the cinnamon, candied peel, rosewater, and dill seeds, if using.

Cut the pastry into 4-inch squares. Place 2 tablespoons of the apple mixture on each square, moisten the edges of the pastry with a little water, and fold over to enclose the apple filling and form a triangle. Press the edges together well to seal. Fry the turnovers in ½-inch deep hot oil, until puffed up and golden. Drain on absorbent paper towels and serve hot, sprinkled with sugar.

Apple Dice with Crisp Croûtons

This is inspired by a recipe from a very old English cookery book and is unusual and distinctive. The soft, translucent cooked apples make an excellent contrast to the crunchy croûtons.

SERVES 4

¼ cup sugar

6 medium apples, peeled and cored

½ stick butter or margarine

3 slices day-old bread, crusts removed and cut into small cubes

1–2 tablespoons Demerara sugar

plain yogurt or *crème fraîche*, to serve

Place the sugar in a medium-sized bowl. Cut the apples into dice and add to the sugar. Toss to coat well. Melt half of the butter or margarine in a heavy skillet, and toss the sugared apples over a medium heat, stirring, until they go a golden brown color and the texture is sticky. Remove and put on a warm platter.

Add the rest of the butter or margarine to the pan, and more if necessary, and sauté the bread cubes so that they mop up the juices and caramel from the apples. When they are crisp all over, toss over the apples, and serve immediately, sprinkled with Demerara sugar. Pass a bowl of *crème fraîche* or plain yogurt to serve.

Drying APPLES

Peel and core as many apples as required, then thinly slice crosswise to make rings. As you go, put the rings into salted water (⅛ cup salt per 3½ cups water) so that they don't discolor.

Drain and dry thoroughly on a towel. Place on wire racks and let dry out in a very low 250°F oven with the door left open. The time taken will vary with the water content of the fruit. When the apple rings are ready, they will become slightly leathery and barely crisp to the touch.

Then cool them thoroughly and pack into wax or parchment paper bags—but not plastic bags, as these will encourage mold.

Alternatively, you can string the apple rings up and hang them over a boiler or gas or wood burning stove to dry. Move them around from time to time so that every surface has a chance to dry out completely.

To use dried apples, soak them in warm water for an hour or so to rehydrate them. Wipe dry and they are then ready to use.

Stuffed Apple Dumplings *Stuffing apples with blackberries is an inspiration, and wrapping them in a light pastry casing makes a fall dessert to remember.*

SERVES 4

4 large tart baking apples

½ lb blackberries, washed and hulled, or

   golden raisins (or both)

2 tablespoons sugar

a little butter or margarine

1½ recipe quantities Sweet Crust Dough (see

   page 150)

beaten egg, to glaze

Crème Anglaise (see page 153), to serve

Peel and core the apples, and hollow out the centers a little to make cavities for the fruit. Roll the blackberries or golden raisins (or mixture of both) in a little sugar, and pack them lightly into the cavities. Top with pats of butter or margarine.

Roll out the dough thinly and cut into 4 squares, each large enough to encase an apple. Put one apple into the center of each dough square, draw up the corners, and pinch them together over the top of the fruit. Dampen and pinch the open edges together. Brush with beaten egg, and place in a greased baking dish. Bake in a preheated oven at 350°F for 25–30 minutes, until the pastry is golden and the apple inside soft. Serve with *Crème Anglaise*.

Apple Macaroons *There is a tradition in Brittany that the apple pickers leave one last and best apple on the end of the highest branch. If it is still there after leaf-fall, there will be a good crop in the orchard the following year. Whether the crop is light or heavy, this dessert is exceptionally good—different in style and delicate in flavor.*

SERVES 6

1 lb apples, peeled, cored, and chopped

½ cup sugar

1 cup dry white wine

½ stick butter or margarine

juice and grated rind of ½ lemon

4 egg yolks

1 cup small macaroons, crushed to coarse crumbs

whipped cream, to serve

Stew the apples with the sugar and wine until you have a thick, smooth purée, stirring frequently. Cool a little. Mix in the butter or margarine, and the lemon juice and rind, and leave until almost cold. Beat the egg yolks thoroughly, and stir them in. Fold in the crushed macaroons. Place in a greased baking dish.

Bake in a preheated oven at 350°F for 40 minutes until firm in the center. Let stand for at least 15 minutes before serving. Serve warm, with whipped cream, or cold just as it is.

Pears

There are about 5,000 named varieties of pear, a native of eastern Europe and the Middle East, of which between twenty and thirty are cultivated on a large scale.

The Williams is the emperor of its species. It is set off by good-quality cheese (with a special affinity for blue cheeses), and is as wonderful in salad as in classic fruit tart. Baking pears in red wine has become a classic recipe (see page 17), and the liqueur *Poire Williams* is of the finest flavor and delicacy.

The pear came into its own in the seventeenth century in France, which became the main country for pear cultivation and cookery. The Comice pear, "Doyenne du Comice," was raised in Angers, the capital of Anjou, and although the original garden has long since disappeared, Comice pears are still widely grown there.

It is best to pick or buy pears firm, then allow them to ripen in the house. When they do, store them in the fridge, since they quickly lose that perfection of texture, which is evident at their peak condition. The supreme pear, the Williams, however, has to be eaten at its point of perfect ripeness. This wonderful fruit, the culmination of 2,000 years of cultivation, has a peak moment in its development, which, when captured, offers a memorable gastronomic experience. Some enthusiasts have been reported as getting up at three in the morning in order to seize this moment of perfection!

Pears in VINE LEAVES

A SIXTEENTH-CENTURY RECIPE: *Lay a layer of vine leaves in an earthen pot, and over them peeled and halved pears. Repeat layers until the pot be full, putting some fine sliced ginger, and a few cloves, between each layer. Fill up the pot with as much cider as the pot will hold, and lay some dish or board upon the pears that they do not swim, and cover the pot closely, and stew all night when the fire be low.*

Let the pears cool in the pot, and serve cold with cream or custard.

Eliza Acton's Pear Meringue *This pudding is extremely successful when made with Bosc pears, the hard pears that cook up so well—they retain their crispness and do not go mushy. Flavor the pears with a little cinnamon or a few cloves if you like, for added interest to this simple but lovely dessert.*

SERVES 4

1½ lb pears, cored and sliced

2 tablespoons soft brown sugar

5 egg whites

5 tablespoons white sugar

Cut the pear slices into 1-inch lengths. Put into a shallow baking dish with a little water, and sprinkle with the sugar. Cover the dish and bake in a preheated oven at 325°F for 15 minutes until the pears are softened. This will depend on the ripeness of the fruit. Let cool.

Whisk the egg whites until very stiff, then fold in the white sugar carefully and lightly. Pile this meringue mixture on top of the pears, and bake in the bottom of a preheated oven at 325°F for 30 minutes. Cool for a few minutes before serving. This dish is also delicious cold.

Poires au Gratin *A simple fruit dessert for summer, when pears are at their best, this mixture of pears stewed with white wine and apricot jam, and covered with a crust of macaroon crumbs, is delightful.*

SERVES 6

2 lb fresh ripe pears, peeled, cored, and
  quartered

⅓ cup dry white wine

⅓ cup apricot jam, strained

1½ cups macaroons, crushed

⅓ stick butter or margarine, cut into tiny dice

Crème Anglaise (see page 153) or plain yogurt, to
  serve

Slice the prepared pears, and arrange them overlapping in a dish. Heat the wine and strained apricot jam together, and pour over the pears. Sprinkle the macaroon crumbs over the top, and dot with the butter or margarine. Bake at 400°F for 20–30 minutes, until the top is lightly browned. Serve hot, warm, or cold with *Crème Anglaise* or plain yogurt.

French Pear Tart *This tart is simplicity itself to make and, I have to admit, one of my favorite desserts. The flavors emerge so pure and uncomplicated, and the tart is so fresh and immediate, that it is a winner every time.*

SERVES 6

1 recipe quantity Sweet Crust Dough (see page 150)

2 large pears, peeled, cored, and sliced

1 egg and 1 egg yolk

3 tablespoons sugar

1 tablespoon cornstarch

½ cup light cream

2 teaspoons vanilla extract

Roll out the dough, and use to line a greased 9 in tart pan. Bake blind (see page 152) in a preheated oven at 375°F for 15 minutes. Cool a little on a wire rack.

Arrange the sliced pears in the cooled tart shell. Beat the egg and egg yolk with the sugar until thick, then beat in the cornstarch, cream, and vanilla extract. Pour over the fruit in the pastry shell.

Bake in the oven at 375°F for 30–40 minutes, or until puffed and golden, and lightly set in the center. Serve hot, warm, or cold.

Pears Baked with Red Wine *Pears baked in red wine has become a cookery classic. A miraculous transformation occurs with the slow cooking of the fruit in the wine: The texture is wonderful and the flavor sublime. Serve this dish either warm or cold, plain as it is, or with thick plain yogurt or* Crème Anglaise *(see page 153).*

SERVES 6

6 large pears, preferably Williams, peeled, cored, and halved

rind of 1 lemon, cut into thin strips

4–6 tablespoons brown sugar

2 cups red wine

Place the pears, overlapping slightly, in a large shallow ovenproof dish. Scatter the lemon rind over the top, and sprinkle with sugar. Pour water over to nearly cover, then add enough wine to immerse the pears. Cover tightly with aluminum foil, and bake slowly at 300°F for about 2 hours until the pears are perfectly tender, turning them halfway through the cooking.

Quinces

The quince is a native of western Asia, and is the "golden apple" of Greek mythology, the prize for a beauty contest, judged by Paris, between Athena, Hera, and Aphrodite. The latter emerged triumphant, endowing her prize with the symbolism of love, marriage, and fertility. Aphrodite is often represented with a quince in her hand, and there was a popular custom in ancient Greece that a bride should eat a quince before entering her nuptial bed. Honey from quince blossom is exceptionally aromatic.

> The medlar and the quince's globe of gold
>
> How rich and fat those yellow fruits do hang!
>
> *The Garden*, Vita Sackville-West, 1946

Quince Honey

Golden and pear-shaped, and with a unique fragrance, the quince makes a beautiful preserve, much enjoyed in medieval times and still just as wonderful today. This recipe is based on one from a twelfth century manuscript which had been translated from the Greek for King Edgar (c. AD 950), who is said to have imported quinces and introduced them to the Britons.

MAKES 1½ LB

1 cup honey

⅓ cup water

1 lb quinces

a small piece of root ginger, peeled and finely grated (optional)

Place the honey and water in a saucepan and cook over medium heat until you have a fairly thick syrup. Chop the quinces small, and boil them in the honey syrup until soft, about 45 minutes. Push through a strainer. Return to the pan and bring to a boil again, then simmer fast until the mixture reaches 200°F and forms a clear, dark, rose-colored honey. Add a little finely grated ginger to flavor, if desired, and let cool. Pour into sterilized jars. Cover and seal (see page 145), and store in a dark, cool place. Use the flavored, thick honey on fresh bread or muffins, and enjoy its old-fashioned and truly original quality.

Right: *Quince honey*

Quince Cream
During the sixteenth and seventeenth centuries hundreds of recipes for quinces appeared in cookbooks, and this is an adaptation of one of them. It is a beautiful and unusual cream, a stunning rose-pink color, and makes a lovely fall dessert.

SERVES 6

1 lb quinces

sugar to taste

⅛ cup candied peel, chopped

¼ cup candied cherries, sliced

1 cup *crème fraîche* or plain yogurt

Cut up the quinces, place in a saucepan with enough water to cover, and bring to a boil. Lower the heat, cover, and simmer for about 40 minutes until they turn to pink mush. Let cool for several hours or overnight (the seeds give out a lot of "jelly").

Push the pulp through a strainer, then sweeten to taste with sugar. Fold in the candied peel and cherries, pour into a bowl, and chill. Just before it sets, stir in the *crème fraîche* or plain yogurt. Pour into a mold and chill for 5–6 hours or overnight.

To turn out, dip briefly into hot water, invert onto a large serving plate, and tap the bottom sharply until the mold comes off.

Cotignac
Cotignac has a taste and texture which for me conjure up my childhood. We had an old quince tree in the garden, and when there was a good crop, my mother used to make this delectable preserve. It is unusual but well worth the effort, and the investment in a small kitchen scale. The only way to get the proportions right is to use equal weights of sugar and fruit purée. Serve in thick, rich slices, with coeur à la crème *or light cream cheese.*

MAKES 6 LB

4 lb quinces

1 cup water

sugar

Cut up the quinces. Put them into a heavy pan with the water. Bring to a boil, and simmer until the fruit is tender. When very soft, mash with a potato masher, then push through a strainer. Weigh the purée, and put it back into the pan with an equal weight of sugar. Stir over a gentle heat until the sugar dissolves, then turn the heat up, and boil until the mixture thickens and turns dark red. Stir constantly to avoid burning.

When the purée is really thick, remove the pan from the heat. Pour into sterilized jars, packing it down well. Cover and seal (see page 145), and store in a cool, dark place. To serve, scoop it out and slice into rounds.

Rhubarb

Rhubarb's country of origin is Siberia (the old name for Russia is "Rus," hence its name). It found its way east and became, with its purgative qualities, one of the primary plants used in Chinese medicine. Rhubarb was introduced from Russia to Britain in 1578, and is the first fruit of our spring, its tender young pink stems making succulent fillings for pies and crumbles, and an excellent jam. Its flavor mingles exceptionally well with elderflower, ginger, orange, and also angelica.

Rhubarb Oat Crunch

This makes a perfect finale to a family meal. The crunchy, crumbly oat topping is mouthwatering. Pick the tender, young stalks of the rhubarb for this recipe, rather than older, tougher ones, as their delicate pink does much to enhance the enjoyment of this dish.

SERVES 6

1 lb rhubarb, trimmed and cut into 2-inch lengths

white sugar to taste

½ cup Demerara sugar

4 tablespoons margarine

⅔ cup old-fashioned rolled oats

¼ cup all-purpose flour

2 tablespoons sunflower seeds

plain yogurt or *Crème Anglaise* (see page 153), to serve

Put the rhubarb into an ovenproof dish with a little water, and cover it. Bake in a preheated oven at 325°F for 20–30 minutes, until tender. Alternatively, you can microwave it. Add white sugar to taste. Cool and drain.

Cream the Demerara sugar with the margarine, and mash in the oats. Sift in the flour, and mix well until crumbly. Finally mix in the sunflower seeds.

Spread the topping over the rhubarb in a heatproof dish. Bake in the oven for 30 minutes at 350°F until the topping is lightly browned. Serve with plain yogurt or *Crème Anglaise*.

Plums Plums and greengages, damsons and medlars, add to the abundance of fall's annual harvest from the orchard.

All Plums are under Venus, and are like women, some better and some worse. As there is a great diversity of kinds, so there is in the operation of Plums, for some that are sweet moisten the stomach, and make the belly soluble: Those that are sour quench thirst more, and bind the belly. The moist and waterish do sooner corrupt in the stomach, but the firm do nourish more, and offend less.

Herbal, Nicholas Culpeper, 1653

Plum Pie *A classic of English country cooking, this fruit pie is entirely enclosed in pastry and filled with cinnamon-scented plums and a few chopped walnuts. Use "wet" walnuts if you can, fresh off the tree, since plums and walnuts are in season at the same time. You can also make this pie with greengages and almonds.*

SERVES 4–6

¾ recipe quantity Shortcake Dough (see page 150)

1 lb plums, washed, halved, pitted and chopped

½ cup Demerara sugar

½ cup walnuts, chopped

2 teaspoons ground cinnamon

grated rind of ½ lemon

grated rind of ½ orange

1 tablespoon butter or margarine, cut into small
  cubes

beaten egg, to glaze

plain yogurt or *Crème Anglaise* (see page 153),
  to serve

Roll out two-thirds of the dough, and use to line an 8-inch greased pie dish. Mix the prepared plums with the sugar, walnuts, cinnamon, and grated rinds, and put into the pie shell. Dot with the butter or margarine. Roll out the remaining dough, and use to cover the pie.

Moisten the edges, and press them well together with a fork. With a sharp knife, slice a little hole in the top of the pie. Brush with beaten egg to glaze. Bake in a preheated oven at 375°F for 45–50 minutes. Serve warm, with plain yogurt or *Crème Anglaise*.

Jalousie
When plums hang heavy on the branch, or lie red and gold in the long grass, this melting piece of pâtisserie is definitely one of fall's delights. Serve it with a cup of coffee at any time of day, or as a delicious dessert served with ice cream.

SERVES 4

⅛ lb store-bought puff pastry

½ lb plums, washed, halved, and pitted

sugar to taste

ground cinnamon to taste

⅓ cup walnuts, chopped (optional)

1 egg yolk, beaten

Roll out the pastry, and cut it into two oblongs. Put one on a greased baking sheet, and brush around the rim with water. Slice the plums, and arrange the slices over the surface of the pastry, leaving a margin. Sprinkle with sugar and cinnamon to taste, and chopped walnuts, if using.

Fold the other oblong of pastry in half lengthwise, and cut a series of parallel lines across the middle, leaving a margin. Open out, and lay over the plum slices. Press the edges of the pastry together well. Brush with beaten egg yolk, and bake in a preheated oven at 425°F for 15 minutes. Lower the heat to 350°F, and cook for a further 10 minutes, until well risen and golden and the plums are tender. Cool on a wire rack.

Iced Plum Soufflé
An elegant pièce de resistance, *this lightly frozen, fruit meringue is served ice cold, but still soft enough to spoon easily out of the dish. The sharp taste of ripe plums is an excellent foil to the creaminess of this memorable dessert.*

SERVES 4–6

1 lb Santa Rosa plums, peeled, pitted, and chopped

1 tablespoon lemon juice

4 tablespoons eau-de-vie or Mirabelle (optional)

¾ cup sugar

½ cup water

4 egg whites

1 cup heavy cream, whipped, or

   crème fraîche

Place the chopped plums with the lemon juice and a little added water in a saucepan. Cover, and cook over medium heat until soft. Drain, then purée in a blender or food processor. Check the taste, add more lemon juice if necessary. Stir in the eau-de-vie or Mirabelle, if using.

Dissolve the sugar in the water over low heat. Bring to a boil, and boil until the syrup reaches 225°F, or a little poured onto a cold saucer starts to set.

Beat the egg whites until very stiff peaks form. Pour on the syrup straight from the heat, and continue whisking until the meringue swells into a white cloud.

Fold the whipped cream or *crème fraîche* into the meringue mixture, then fold in the plum purée. Invert into a 4-cup soufflé dish, and leave in the freezer until ready to serve. Serve icy cold, but soft enough to spoon out.

Damson Cheese *Little crooked trees, often mossy, growing along banks and in English country lanes, yield a deep purple, wild plum in early fall. Its name, damson, means the "plum from Damascus," short for the romantic Damascene. Country people made "cheeses" from many wild fruits, and some old damson cheeses are known to have been made a foot high and a foot across, although the average was jam-jar size. Inverted onto a plate, they were sliced, stuck with split almonds, and served with port poured over them.*

YOU WILL NEED: • damsons, washed • sugar

Put the damsons into a baking dish with a little water, and cook in a preheated oven at 325°F for about 30 minutes, until the juices run freely and the pits are loose. Remove and reserve the pits. Put the fruit through a strainer, or purée in a blender or food processor.

Crack open the pits, and remove the kernels. Add them to the fruit pulp, and weigh it. Place in a clean stainless steel pan, and to every 1 lb, add 1 lb sugar. Place over gentle heat, and simmer until a little gels when placed on a saucer (see page 145). Put the "cheese" into sterilized straight-sided jars. Cover and seal (see page 145), and store in a cool, dark place.

Leave for at least six months; it improves with keeping up to 2 years. At its best it will have shrunk a little from the sides of the jar, and the top will be crusted with sugar.

Baked DAMSONS

This simple way of cooking damsons retains all their flavor and color, and it is a wonderful fall dessert.

Pack your damsons into a heatproof dish, cover with sugar, and fill with water to the level of the damsons. Cover closely, and bake in a preheated oven at 350°F until the fruit is soft—about 20 minutes, depending on the ripeness of the fruit. Leave covered until cold to preserve the flavor and serve chilled with *Crème Anglaise* (see page 153).

Very Good Damson Jam
This is an excellent jam, but if you do not have a damson tree, any fresh-picked purple plum will do. It is delicious on English muffins in the fall, eaten sitting by the fire as the evenings draw in.

YOU WILL NEED: • **ripe damsons, freshly gathered and washed** • **water** • **sugar**

Cut the damsons open, and remove the pits. Put them into a saucepan with the water to just cover, and simmer for 40 minutes. Weigh, return to the pan, and stir in half their weight in sugar. Stir over medium heat until the sugar dissolves, and then boil for about 15 minutes, stirring and removing any scum, until the setting point is reached (see page 145). Pot, cover, and seal (see page 145). Store in a cool, dark place.

If you want a very fine jam, strain the fruit before you weigh it.

Greengage and Almond Tart
Greengages have a royal provenance: Claude, queen to François I of France in the early sixteenth century, gave her name to a tree imported from Italy, and she grew it in quantity near her palace at Blois. In the eighteenth century, Sir William Gage brought the "prune de la reine Claude" back from France to England, lost the labels, and called it "green Gage's plum." It has a delicacy all of its own, a special fruit which makes a superb tart with ground almonds and an apricot glaze.

SERVES 6–8

1 recipe quantity Sweet Crust Dough (see page 150)

1 cup ground almonds

1 cup sugar

½ stick butter or margarine, melted

1 egg yolk

4 tablespoons whipping cream

1 tablespoon kirsch (optional)

2 lb greengages, washed, halved, and pitted

½ cup water

3 tablespoons apricot jam

Roll out the dough, and use to line a greased 10-inch tart pan. Bake blind (see page 152) in a preheated oven at 375°F for 15 minutes, until golden and set.

Mix the ground almonds and half the sugar with the melted butter or margarine. Beat in the egg yolk and finally the cream, and kirsch if desired. Spread this mixture over the tart bottom.

Poach the greengages lightly with the remaining sugar and water. When soft, drain, reserving a little of the cooking liquid. Place the greengages carefully over the top of the cream.

Heat the apricot jam with the reserved cooking liquid, and brush the top of the fruit with this glaze. Let set in a cool place.

Greengage (or Plum) Chutney
Whether you use greengages or plums, this chutney makes a wonderful addition to the winter table, and is especially delicious with fresh bread and cheese for a simple lunch.

MAKES 4 LB

2 lb greengages or ripe plums, washed, halved, and
  pitted

½ lb apples, cored and sliced

½ lb onions, peeled and sliced

⅔ cup raisins

¼ lb carrots, peeled or scrubbed, and grated

1 cup Demerara sugar

1 tablespoon salt

1 teaspoon each ground cloves, ginger, and allspice

1 small dried red chili (optional)

2 cups white wine vinegar

Mix the fruits, onions, raisins, grated carrot, and sugar together in a bowl. Put the salt, spices, and chili, if using, into a preserving pan, and pour in the vinegar. Bring slowly to a boil, and then add the fruit mixture. Stir well, bring to a boil again, and simmer steadily, stirring, until the chutney is thick and no pools of liquid remain on the surface. Pour into sterilized jars, making sure that no air bubbles are trapped in the jar. Cover with plastic screw-top lids (see page 145).

Store in a cool, dark, dry place for at least 3 months before using but, as with all chutneys, they are best left for at least a year before eating.

MEDLARS

The medlar looks like a large, rounded rose hip the color of a russet apple, and on the tree it is as hard as a brick. Medlars soften on storing; the *Child's Guide* of 1850 says: "They are kept in moist bran for a fortnight before being rotten enough to eat." In rich households, medlars were kept in a silver dish of moist sawdust on the sideboard.

In England the medlars are gathered in early fall. They are spread out in a single layer and stored in a well-ventilated place for several weeks until they soften. When soft, they are eaten out of hand or the flesh can be scooped out and mixed with a dash of lemon juice or with cream and sugar.

TO ROAST MEDLARS: Arrange softened medlars in a shallow dish, dot with butter, and scatter over a few whole cloves. Bake in a preheated oven at 375°F for 10 minutes. Serve as you would baked apples, with plain yogurt or *Crème Anglaise* (see page 153).

Peaches
The Romans believed that the peach came from Persia, hence its botanical name *Prunus persica*. In fact, it was originally cultivated in China, where peach blossom symbolizes long life, and came to Europe by way of Persia.

Peaches were often grown in Victorian hothouses, trained up against south-facing walls. For dessert, they might be made into a salad: A glass bowl was rinsed round with a little brandy, the fruit sliced into it, and barely covered with champagne and crushed white sugar candy.

Nectarines are more or less interchangeable with peaches, being a plum-skinned, smooth variety of peach. To peel either of them, pour boiling water over them in a bowl, and leave for a few minutes. Then slit the skin with a sharp knife and it will peel off easily.

Pêches Aurore
This is food for the gods: Ripe peaches and a scoop of fresh strawberry ice cream are covered with a layer of thick zabaglione—which tastes like nectar!

SERVES 2

2 large ripe peaches

½ cup sugar

1 cup water

1 teaspoon vanilla extract

2–3 scoops strawberry ice cream, softened slightly

small macaroons, to serve

Zabaglione:

2–3 egg yolks

¼ cup sugar

⅓ cup Marsala or sweet white wine

Peel (see above), halve, and pit the peaches. Make a light syrup by boiling together the sugar and water for a few minutes. Add the vanilla extract to the syrup, then gently poach the peach halves in it for several minutes until tender.

Now prepare the zabaglione. Beat the egg yolks with the sugar in a small bowl until pale, then beat in the wine. Set over a pan of barely simmering water. Whisk steadily with a beater until the mixture thickens and turns pale, about 5–6 minutes. Be very careful not to overheat, otherwise it will curdle, then remove from the pan and whisk until cold.

Place a layer of strawberry ice cream in each individual glass dish, and place the peach halves on top. Coat with the zabaglione, and serve at once with macaroons.

Classic Peach Tart
A great favorite, this simple tart is made of shortcake dough, sprinkled thickly with macaroon crumbs, topped with the fruit, and baked. An apricot glaze is the finishing touch. It is brilliant. This tart freezes well.

SERVES 6

1 recipe quantity Shortcake Dough (see page 150)

¼ lb macaroons, crushed

4–5 ripe peaches, halved, pitted, and sliced

½ cup water

3 tablespoons apricot jam

Roll out the dough, and use to line a greased 9-inch tart pan.

Sprinkle in the macaroon crumbs. Arrange the peach slices in the tart shell in close concentric circles, starting from the outside. Bake in a preheated oven at 425°F for 20–25 minutes, until the tart shell is lightly browned and the fruit softened. Cover with aluminum foil after 15 minutes if the tart begins to brown too deeply.

Heat the water and apricot jam together, and while the tart is still warm, brush it with this glaze. Let cool, and serve warm or cold.

Stuffed Peaches
The simplicity of crushed macaroon crumbs stuffed inside the pit cavity of a ripe peach makes a fresh, light dessert. It is lovely served with very cold Zabaglione (see page 28) or Crème Anglaise *(see page 153).*

SERVES 6–8

6 large peaches, halved and pitted

¼ lb macaroons, crushed

1 large egg yolk, beaten

1 tablespoon sugar

Scoop out a little more around the pit cavity of each peach half to make it larger. Mash the scooped-out peach flesh, and mix it with the macaroon crumbs, egg yolk, and sugar. Pile this mixture back into the pit cavity of each peach half, making a mound. Place the stuffed peach halves in a lightly greased, ovenproof dish, and bake in a preheated oven at 325°F for 40 minutes. Let cool slightly before serving. A perfect dessert for a summer party, served with a sweet wine such as Beaumes de Venise.

Spiced PEACHES

You can make this wonderful preserve by following the recipe for Spiced Apricots on page 30, substituting the fruit.

A p r i c o t s The apricot is a native of China, and has been cultivated

there for over 4,000 years. It also grows abundantly in the Middle East, in Armenia, and around

the Black Sea. The apricot gets its name from the Latin *praecox*, meaning early, because it blos-

soms early in the year—after the almond and before the peach. It is therefore prone to frost,

which is why it does not do well in northerly zones.

Spiced Apricots *I have been making these preserved apricots for many years, and they are one of*
the most outstandingly successful of the range of preserves on my larder shelf. Wonderful with a cheese and French bread,
or on a mixed buffet table, or with a simple salad meal of any kind, they are also delicious with roast chicken, whether hot
or cold—a versatile and popular stand-by all year round.

MAKES 5–6 LB

12 whole cloves

2 x 3 in cinnamon sticks

8 allspice berries

2 cups white distilled vinegar

5 cups sugar

3 lb dried apricots, or 4 lb fresh apricots, halved
  and pitted

Tie all the spices in a cheesecloth bag, and bring to a boil in the vinegar. Add the sugar, and dissolve over low
heat. Add the apricots, and simmer very gently for 5–8 minutes if using fresh, 10–12 minutes if using dried.
Then lift the fruit out with a slotted spoon, and pack into warm, sterilized jars. Boil the liquid until it reduces
to a thick syrup, pour over the apricots in the jars, then cover and seal (see page 145).

Apricot TART

You can make a classic apricot tart in the
same way as the French Pear Tart on page
17, substituting ripe apricots, halved and
pitted, for pear slices.

Right: *Spiced apricots*

Apricot FOOL

The fruit fool is an English invention, and there are many variations on the theme. Basically, the fool is a fruit purée with either cream or *Crème Anglaise* (see page 153) added, which is spooned into glasses and served chilled. Roughly speaking, the ratio of purée to cream or *Crème Anglaise* is half and half—you will find your own preference. Sweeten your purée according to taste, and if you wish, you can add a little sugar to enhance its flavor. Fruit fools are also successfully made replacing the cream or *Crème Anglaise* with plain yogurt.

To MAKE PURÉE: Halve and pit the apricots if fresh, choosing very ripe ones only. Purée in a blender or food processor with a little orange juice. If using dried apricots, soak them for several hours or overnight, and then purée them with a little of their soaking liquid. Fold the purée into your cream, *Crème Anglaise*, or whole-milk, plain yogurt, spoon into glasses, and serve well chilled.

See also Gooseberry Fool on page 47.

Hunza Jam *Hunzas are the little, round, pale dried apricots that come from the Hunza valley in the Himalayas. Their flavor is delectable but they are difficult to obtain. You can also make this using ordinary dried apricots but the results will be different. Stir in ½ cup blanched, slivered almonds at the end of cooking to give the flavor a little boost.*

MAKES 1½ LB:

¾ lb dried hunza apricots

1½ cups sugar

Soak the apricots in water to cover until quite soft. Cook them in their soaking water until pulpy, about 10–15 minutes, then cool. If using Hunzas, remove the pits, crack them open with a pestle, and remove and retain the nutty kernels.

Return the apricots to the pan, stir in the sugar, and cook over low heat until the sugar dissolves. Then boil gently to setting point (see page 145). Let stand for a little, stir in the inner kernels or almonds if using, then pour into warm, sterilized jars. Cover and seal (see page 145). Store in a cool, dark place.

Apricot and Almond Crumble
This is a wonderful British dessert for summer, excellent family food with a hint of luxury and a touch of the exotic. Out of season, I use dried, unsulfured apricots, which are by far the best in flavor; they are mouthwatering in this recipe.

SERVES 4–6

18–20 large ripe apricots, halved and pitted

sugar to taste

½ cup blanched slivered almonds

plain yogurt or *Crème Anglaise* (see page 153), to
  serve

Crumble Topping:

1 cup all-purpose flour

½ cup sugar

¾ cup ground almonds

1 stick butter or margarine

a few drops almond extract

Cut the apricots into quarters. Arrange the apricot quarters in a large, shallow ovenproof dish, and sprinkle with sugar to taste.

To make the crumble topping, mix the flour, sugar, and ground almonds together, then rub in the butter or margarine until crumbly. Mix in the almond extract. Spread over the fruit, and sprinkle with the slivered almonds.

Bake in a preheated oven at 400°F for about 35 minutes, until nicely browned. If the almonds begin to brown too much, turn the heat down to 350°F. Serve hot or warm, with plain yogurt or *Crème Anglaise*.

Eighteenth-Century APRICOT ICE CREAM

An inimitable ice cream is easily made following this old recipe (although, obviously, our freezing techniques are somewhat different!).

TO MAKE ICE CREAM: *Peel, pit, and scald twelve apricots, beat them in a fine mortar, and put to them ¾ cup of sugar and 2 cups of scalding cream. Work it through a fine strainer, put it into a can that hath a close cover, and set it in a tub of ice broken small and a large quantity of salt put among it. When you see your cream grow thick around the edges, stir it, and set it in again until it is all frozen up. Then put on the lid and have ready another tub with ice and salt as before: Put your can in the middle and lay ice over and under it: Let it stand four or five hours, and then dip your can in warm water before you invert it. You may use any sort of fruit if you have not apricots, only observe to work it fine.*

The Experienced English Housekeeper, Elizabeth Raffald, 1769

Apricot Shortcake *Apricots are one of early summer's most delectable treats, and this scrumptious dessert, for all its simplicity, is extremely more-ish. There will never be any leftovers!*

SERVES 3–4

¾ lb fresh ripe apricots, halved and pitted

2 tablespoons sugar

1 cup all-purpose flour

½ teaspoon baking powder

3 tablespoons butter or margarine

⅓ cup light brown sugar

vanilla ice cream or *Crème Anglaise* (see page 153), to serve

Put the apricots into an ovenproof dish or cake pan, and sprinkle with the sugar.

Sift the flour with the baking powder, and rub in the butter or margarine until the mixture is crumbly. Stir in the brown sugar, and mix well. Press the mixture down on top of the fruit with a fork.

Bake in a preheated oven at 350°F for 25–30 minutes, until the top is pale golden. Serve hot, warm, or cold—whichever way, it is quite irresistible—with vanilla ice cream or *Crème Anglaise*.

Apricot Bavaroise *This classic French dessert shows up apricots at their very best, as one of our finest fruits. This is a dinner-party piece. Use well-ripened apricots, neither too hard nor too mushy. They should be just firm to the touch with a strong golden color as these will be the sweetest.*

SERVES 4–6

¾ lb ripe apricots, halved and pitted

1½ tablespoons powdered gelatin

6 tablespoons very hot water

1 cup whipping cream or *crème fraîche*

1 tablespoon confectioners' sugar

a little lemon juice (optional)

a few shelled pistachio nuts, to decorate

Purée the apricots in a blender or food processor. Dissolve the gelatin in the hot water, then add to the apricots in the blender, and process again to mix in. Beat the cream or *crème fraîche* with the confectioners' sugar, and when it is stiff, fold the apricot purée into it. Taste, and add more sugar and a little lemon juice if required. Pour into a lightly oiled, decorative mold. Chill in the refrigerator, preferably overnight, until set.

Invert, lift off mold, and scatter a few pistachio nuts over the top and around the edge just before serving.

Figs

The fig was one of the earliest fruit trees to be cultivated by primitive man, and it is believed to have originated in the Near East, before spreading to the Mediterranean, India, China and the Americas. Before the development of refined sugar, figs were made into a syrup, with dates and honey, and used as a sweetener. There are two kinds of fig trees: One produces fruit twice a year, ususally in June and September, and the other bears fruit once, in the Fall.

> Do men gather grapes of thorns, or figs of thistles?
>
> St Matthew's Gospel 7:16

Fig Jam

If you are fortunate enough to have a fig tree that bears ripe figs, why bother to cook them? I always wonder. They are exquisite just as they are; nothing can improve on them except possibly the indulgence of heavy cream. But if you ever have more than you can eat, and they are dropping off the tree, make this jam. It is a masterpiece, and both breakfast and desserts are transformed by it.

MAKES 4 LB

3 lb figs

3 cups sugar

juice and grated rind of 2 lemons

Wipe the figs clean, remove the stems, and then chop them roughly. Put into the top part of a double-boiler and cover with the sugar. Add a little water to moisten. Cover with a lid, and cook over boiling water for 30–40 minutes, until the sugar has dissolved and the fruit is quite soft.

Transfer the mixture to a preserving pan, and add the lemon rind and juice, stirring well. Bring to a boil, and boil rapidly for about 8–10 minutes, stirring, until the jam thickens and reaches setting point (see page 145). Pour into warm, sterilized jars, cover, and seal (see page 145). Store in a cool, dark place.

Strawberries A beautiful and kind young girl, according to

the Brothers Grimm, was driven out by her stepmother to find strawberries in the snow. Lost in the forest, she came across a dwarves' house, and shared her crust of bread with them. They offered her shelter, and as she swept the snow aside from the doorway with their broom, she found strawberries growing.

The image of the red fruit in the snow in the dark forest is a compelling one. The strawberry, a member of the rose family, has a particular attraction: Its color is wonderful, and it is unique among fruits in having the seeds dotted around on the outside rather than embedded within.

Strawberry Shortcake *Strawberry shortcake is one of summer's great treats, with its layers of crumbly biscuit, whipped cream, and juicy strawberries. A wonderful dessert for a meal alfresco, lingering over its flavors in the sunshine.*

SERVES 6

3 cups flour, half wholewheat and half all-purpose

1 teaspoon baking powder

2 sticks butter or margarine

¾ cup light brown sugar

1½ lb strawberries, washed and hulled

sugar

1½ cups heavy cream, whipped

Sift the flour with the baking powder, and rub in the butter or margarine until the mixture resembles fine bread crumbs. Mix in the sugar to combine. Press the mixture into two 8-inch buttered layer pans, and bake in a preheated oven at 325°F for 30–40 minutes, until a light golden color. Cool in the pans before inverting.

Slice the strawberries, reserving a few whole ones for decoration, and toss the slices in sugar. Place half of them on top of one of the shortcake layers, and cover with a thick layer of whipped cream. Top with the other layer of shortcake. Cover the top with another layer of sliced strawberries, then a layer of whipped cream, and decorate with the reserved whole strawberries. Keep in a cool place until ready to serve.

Strawberries in Cream *This is a superb way to serve strawberries, but it comes with a warning:* "Raw cream, eaten with strawberries, is a rural man's banquet: Yet I have known such banquets hath put men in jeopardy of their lives, by the excess thereof."

Dietary of Health, Andrew Boorde, 1547

SERVES 4

1½ cups heavy cream or *crème fraîche*

1½ lb strawberries, washed and hulled

confectioners' sugar, to dust

Whip the cream or *crème fraîche* lightly. Cut the larger strawberries in half, leaving the small ones whole. Drop into the cream, stirring and mashing lightly, until the cream won't hold any more fruit. It will be a wonderful pale pink color. Sprinkle with a dusting of confectioners' sugar and serve forth, in June, on a green lawn, under shady trees by the river.

This also works beautifully as a filling for a light sponge cake.

Strawberry Jam *At the height of the strawberry season each year, I make this very simple jam, which never lasts long because it is so popular. It is unbeatable on freshly made biscuits for a summery treat in the garden, and also makes an excellent filling for sponge cake.*

MAKES 5 LB

3 lb strawberries, washed and hulled

4½ cups preserving sugar

2 thick slices of lemon

Put all the ingredients into a preserving pan with a little water, and simply boil to setting point (see page 145). Remove the slices of lemon, and put the jam into warm, sterilized jars. Cover and seal (see page 145), and store in a dark, cool place.

Strawberry SAUCE

You can make the simplest of strawberry sauces to go with ice cream or with fresh peaches, for example. It freezes well, and is one of the best ways of saving these berries for the winter months. Simply purée washed, hulled strawberries with a little sugar to taste in a blender or food processor until smooth. Strain through a tightly woven metal strainer to remove the seeds, and add a little orange-flower water if you wish for an exotic touch.

A *tart of* STRAWBERRIES

Pick and wash your Strawberries clean, and put them in the pastry one by another, as thick as you can. Then take Sugar, Cinnamon and a little Ginger finely beaten, and well mingled together, and cast them on the strawberries. Cover them with the lid finely cut into Lozenges, and so let them bake a quarter of an hour.

A Book of Fruits and Flowers, Thomas Jenner, 1653

English Summer Pudding

The most English of recipes, Summer Pudding is one of high summer's peak culinary experiences, and not at all what Americans think of when they hear "pudding" . Old English recipes made frequent use of bread, usually resulting in rather heavy dishes, but this is quite wonderful, and is a masterpiece of English country cooking.

SERVES 6

¾ lb strawberries, washed, hulled, and halved

½ lb raspberries, washed and hulled

½ lb black currants or red currants, cleaned

¼ lb cherries, halved and pitted

5 tablespoons water

6 tablespoons sugar

10–12 slices wholewheat bread

Crème Anglaise (see page 153) or plain yogurt, to serve

Place all the prepared fruits in a large pan with the water. Stir over gentle heat until well mixed, then simmer gently for about 5 minutes. Stir in the sugar, remove from the heat, and let cool.

Butter a 7-inch cake pan or 3-cup ovenproof bowl. Trim the crusts from the bread. Cut some of the slices in half lengthwise, and use to line the sides of the pan or bowl. Cut more of the slices into triangles, and use to line the bottom of the pan or bowl, making sure that the edges fit neatly together. Fill with the fruit and enough of the juice to moisten the bread, including around the sides. Cover the top with more bread triangles, and pour over more juice, making sure that every bit of bread is moistened.

Place a flat plate over the pudding to weight it down, and leave overnight. To serve, invert onto a serving dish, and pass *Crème Anglaise* or plain yogurt around to go with it.

Raspberries
Some gardeners claim that yellow raspberries have a superior flavor, mild and sweet, but whatever the color many think the best way to eat them is fresh off the vine with thick cream and sugar. Back in the seventeenth century, British garden-lover and botanist John Parkinson called this an "afternoon dish" in summertime; and so it still is. Raspberries freeze quite well whole, but to my mind the best way to store them for the winter is in the form of a purée, strained and sweetened to taste—a delicious sauce with ice cream.

Raspberry Jam
Raspberries have a high pectin content, and therefore make a well-set jam, one of the season's best. This is a treat through the winter months when summer is but a memory.

MAKES 5 LB

3 lb raspberries, washed and hulled

4½ cups sugar

Toss the raspberries in the sugar in a big bowl, and leave in the sun until warmed through (this is advice from an old country cook book). Then slide the fruit and the juice that has formed into a pan, bring to a boil, and cook rapidly to setting point (see page 145). Can while still hot, and seal in the jars (see page 145).

A *Seventeenth-Century* RASPBERRY CREAM

Old-fashioned country "creams" were in most cases fruit blended into a base of plain whipped cream, sometimes lightened with beaten egg white. The color of this one is beautiful: A clear "apple blossom" effect. And the addition of rosewater is seductive:

When you have whipt your cream, sweeten it, and take two ladlefuls (only) and bruise the raspberries into it, and season with rose-water, and again whip it well, and then put it to your [main] cream, and, stirring all together, dish it up.

Ms of c.1700

Raspberry Vinegar
This is a "must" for a well-stocked larder shelf. You can use it in salad dressings all year round, and in delicately flavored sauces. It is wonderful, and very easy to make.

MAKES 10 CUPS

1½ lb raspberries, washed and hulled

4 cups malt vinegar

4½ cups sugar

Cover the raspberries with water, and simmer for 30 minutes. Strain off the juice into a large pan—there will be about 4 cups. Add the vinegar and sugar to the juice, and stir all together as it heats through. Bring to a boil, and simmer for 15–20 minutes, until the liquid becomes syrupy.

Pour into clean wine bottles and cork. Store in a cool, dark place.

Summer Trifle
This great classic of English cooking lends itself to improvisation with whatever fruits are in season. Traditionally, sherry was used to moisten the sponge cake.

SERVES 6–8

18-20 lady fingers

½ cup tropical fruit juice, or half and half with white
  wine

2½ lb mixed summer fruits, such as
  raspberries, strawberries, peaches, mangoes, kiwi
  fruit, grapes, etc., prepared and sliced as necessary

3 tablespoons sugar

2 cups thick custard sauce or *Crème Anglaise*
  (see page 153)

2 cups plain yogurt

Break the lady fingers in half and lay one third of them in the bottom of an attractive 8-inch glass dish. Sprinkle one third of the tropical fruit juice or mixture of wine and juice over them, and set aside. Mix the prepared fruits with the sugar in another bowl, reserving a few raspberries and strawberries for decoration. Spoon half of the fruit with its juice over the sponges, and then repeat the layers, ending with a layer of sponge cake fingers moistened with the last of the juice.

Mix the custard sauce or *Crème Anglaise* with the plain yogurt, and spread it over the top. Chill overnight. Decorate with the reserved raspberries and strawberries, and serve.

Raspberry WATER ICE
Follow the recipe for Red or White Currant Water Ice on page 42, using 2½ lb raspberries, washed and hulled, instead of the mixture of currants and raspberries.

Currants Black, red, and white currants are members of the Ribes
family and native to northern latitudes. The black currant, with its heavily scented leaves,
grows wild across the whole of Europe and northern Asia. Its high vitamin content is greatly
valued, and the shrub is now farmed extensively.

Red and white currants are found mainly by streams and in wet woodlands. The
Scandinavians and Russians cultivate the red currant widely and it is a popular ingredient
in their cooking. The white currant has its own distinctive flavor and is slightly less acidic
than the red.

Red or White Currant Water Ice *Seventeenth-century British cooks used
to make little red currant creams (a version of syllabub without the wine), and a fool made with red currant juice was also
popular. Sir Kenelm Digby recommended in 1669 that the red currants be "fresh gathered" in the morning. This water
ice is yet another delectable way of cooking with red currants, and makes an elegant dessert for a summer dinner party.*

SERVES 4–6

¾ cup sugar

½ cup water

2¼ lb ripe red or white currants, washed and
  stripped from their stalks

½ lb raspberries, washed and hulled

lemon juice to taste

Boil the sugar with the water for 6–8 minutes until syrupy. Purée the red or white currants and raspberries in
a blender or food processor, and then pass through a strainer. Mix the resulting purée with the syrup, then add
lemon juice to taste. Pour into a freezer container, cover, and freeze for 1 hour, or until the edges begin to harden. Scoop out, and blend until smooth, then return to the freezer to complete the freezing. Alternatively, put
the mixture into an ice-cream maker, and follow the manufacturer's instructions for freezing.

To convert this recipe into ice cream, purée the fruit but do not strain. Then mix with sugar to sweeten to
taste, or with syrup as above, and blend gradually with 2 pints "fresh sweet cream" (i.e., *crème fraîche*), adding
lemon juice only if desired. Fold in a beaten egg white, and freeze as above.

Blackcurrant JELLY

Black currants gel very easily when ripe. The rich, thick juice of a deep, dark color is, according to Eliza Acton (1840), "useful in illness" and very refreshing.

If you have a juicer, treat yourself to this elixir of midsummer. To make black currant jelly, follow the instructions for making jellies on page 146. Using 2 lb fruit to 1 cup water, cover the pan and simmer for 30 minutes. Cool, then strain through a jelly bag.

To every 2 cups juice add 1½ cups sugar. Stir over gentle heat until the sugar has dissolved. Bring to a boil and boil rapidly to setting point, about 10 minutes. Remove scum as it arises.

Pour into warm, sterilized jars. Cover and seal (see page 145).

Black Currant Flan *Based on the classic French technique of making fruit flans, this is hugely successful as a dessert for midsummer. The rich, slightly tart flavor of the black currants makes a mouthwatering contrast to the* Crème Pâtissière *which lines a crisp pastry shell.*

SERVES 4–6

1½ recipe quantities Sweet Crust Dough (see page 150)

1 recipe quantity *Crème Pâtissière* (see page 153)

1½ lb black currants, washed and cleaned

¼ cup sugar

4 tablespoons apricot jam

crème fraîche or yogurt, to serve (optional)

Roll out the dough, and use to line a 10-inch greased flan or pie pan. Bake blind (see page 152) in a preheated oven at 375°F for 20 minutes, until golden and firm. Cool. Spread the bottom with the *Crème Pâtissière*.

Put the prepared black currants into a pan with the sugar, and heat gently, stirring carefully, for 3–4 minutes until the currants have softened slightly and the juice runs. Let cool in the pan, then strain off the juice, reserving it. Lay the currants over the *Crème Pâtissière*. Heat the apricot jam, adding enough of the reserved black currant juice to make a pouring consistency, and pass it through a strainer. Trickle it over the black currants. Let cool, and serve well chilled, with *crème fraîche* or yogurt, if desired.

Black Currant Clafoutis

Family food from the French, a clafoutis *consists of fresh fruit baked in a batter mixture. It rises to turn golden brown during cooking, while the fruit inside melts in the mouth.*

SERVES 6

1 cup milk

¼ cup sugar

3 eggs

1 teaspoon vanilla extract

pinch of salt

1 cup flour, sifted

1 lb black currants

¼ cup confectioners' sugar

plain Greek yogurt, to serve

Put all the ingredients except the fruit and confectioners' sugar in a blender or food processor, and blend for 2 minutes to form a smooth batter. Pour a ¼-inch layer of batter into the bottom of a greased 8-inch square metal heat proof dish, and place over moderate heat for a minute or so, swirling it around until a film of batter has set in the bottom of the dish. Be careful not to let it burn. Remove from heat.

Spread the black currants over the film of batter, and sprinkle on the confectioners' sugar. Pour on the rest of the batter, place in the middle of a preheated oven, and bake at 350°F for 50–60 minutes, until puffed and brown, and when a sharp knife plunged into the center comes out clean. Serve hot or warm (it will sink if not served immediately) with plain yogurt.

The Queen's SWEETMEAT

This appears to be a jelly of red currant and raspberry with whole cherries set in it. It sounds very special—worth a try if you are an inventive cook:

MARMULATE OF CHERRIES WITH JUICE OF RASPBERRIES AND CURRANTS: *Mingle juice of Rasps and red Currants with the stoned Cherries, and boil this mixture into Marmulate, with a quarter or at most a third part of Sugar ... Madam Plancy (who maketh this sweetmeat for the Queen) useth this proportion. Take three pounds of Cherries pitted: Half a pound of clear juice of Raspes, and one pound of the juice of Red Currants, with one pound of fine Sugar. Put them all together in the preserving pan; boil them with a quick fire, especially at the first, skimming them all the while as any scum riseth. When you find them of a fit consistence, with a fine clear jelly mingled with the Cherries, take the preserving pan from the fire and bruise the Cherries with the back of your preserving spoon: Put them up when they are of a fit temper of coolness, peradventure, to keep all the year, there may be requisite a little more Sugar.*

The Closet of Sir Kenelm Digby Opened, 1669

Gooseberries

The gooseberry is the first of Britain's soft fruits to appear in the summer garden, and a gooseberry pie was traditionally served up at Whitsun celebrations in May. There is an old English recipe for such a pie in which the fruit and sugar are encased in a raised-pie crust—a sweet version of a pork-pie crust— and when cooked, melted apple jelly was poured in through a slit in the lid. The pie was then left to set and gel. Other typically English recipes using gooseberries were for cakes, puddings, fools, and jams, dishes which have stood the test of time and which are a distinctive part of English country cooking. Don't pick gooseberries too early in the season, though: Unripe gooseberries are very sour and need a chance to sun ripen.

Whitsuntide Gooseberry Pie

Whitsuntide used to be a major English festival, with a Whitsun King and Queen chosen to preside over the fun. All over the land, parishioners gathered for various social events, and the first of the Morris dancers made their appearance in their ribbons and bells. The Sunday feast would end with a magnificent gooseberry pie.

SERVES 4–6

1½ lb gooseberries, cleaned

4–6 tablespoons sugar

⅔ recipe quantity Sweet Crust Dough (see page 150)

1 egg white, beaten

plain yogurt or *Crème Anglaise* (see page 153), to serve

Put the gooseberries into a large, shallow pie dish, and toss them in the sugar. Place an inverted egg cup in the center. Roll out the dough ¼ inch thick, and cut it to fit over the top with a margin of about ⅜ inch. Moisten the rim of the dish, and place the dough over the top. Press down the edges with a fork, and make a small slit in the center above the egg cup. Decorate with dough "leaves" if you like, moistening the undersides of the "leaves" before pressing them down. Brush with beaten egg white, and bake in a preheated oven at 350°F for 25–30 minutes, until the crust is set and turns a light golden color. Serve hot, with lots of plain yogurt or *Crème Anglaise*.

Gooseberry Fool *Quintessentially English, the gooseberry fool is a delicate dish of subtle flavor, and an inimitable pale green color. You can make it with cream or custard sauce, depending on how rich you want it; or with plain yogurt for a tangier flavor. If gooseberries are difficult to obtain, you could also make this with the same quantity of blueberries or raspberries, cooked in the microwave.*

SERVES 4

1 lb gooseberries, cleaned

1 tablespoon butter

sugar to taste

1 cup whipping cream, whole-milk, plain yogurt or
   custard sauce

thin, crisp cookies, to serve

Put the gooseberries into an ovenproof dish with a little water, cover with a lid, and bake in a preheated oven at 325°F, until completely soft and pulpy, about 40–45 minutes. Alternatively, you can microwave them. While they are still hot, stir in the butter and enough sugar to sweeten. Cool, then purée in a blender or food processor. Strain them if you want a very fine fool.

Whip the cream, if using, to the same consistency as the fool, or use whole-milk plain yogurt or custard sauce, and fold it softly into the purée. Spoon into glasses, and chill thoroughly. Serve with thin, crisp cookies.

Gooseberry and Mint Compote *The name "gooseberry" means "crisp berry," and the shrub grows successfully only in fairly northerly climes. They have therefore not been much used in European cuisines, but the British have many traditional recipes which make use of them. This one links the gooseberry with fresh mint, two distinctly compatible flavors.*

SERVES 3–4

½ cup sugar

1 cup water

1 lb gooseberries, cleaned

several sprigs fresh mint, tied in a cheesecloth bag

fresh mint, to garnish

crisp cookies, to serve

Make a syrup by dissolving the sugar in the water and boiling for 5 minutes. Add the gooseberries to the syrup, with the mint, and cook very gently for 10 minutes, partially covered. Remove the mint and cool the gooseberries. Chill. Serve in glass bowls, garnished with mint and delicate crisp cookies to hand around.

Gooseberry, Red Currant and Thyme Jam *The addition*

of fresh thyme gives this preserve a unique flavor. A wonderful summer jam, it is excellent on freshly baked bread or biscuits, and delicious as a filling for a plain sponge cake.

MAKES 7 LB

2 lb gooseberries, cleaned

1 lb red currants

4 cups water

small bunch of fresh thyme tied in a cheesecloth bag

8 cups sugar

Simmer the gooseberries and red currants in the water with the bag of thyme for 30 minutes. Remove the thyme, add the sugar, and stir until dissolved. Boil to setting point (see page 145). Pour in warm, sterilized jars, cover, and seal (see page 145). Store in a cool, dark place.

Groseillée *This is raspberry and gooseberry jelly which, at a guess from its name, is of French*

inspiration. The French use gooseberries very little in their cooking—perhaps because it is not a native plant —although their gooseberry sauce for mackerel is well known. This combination of fruits, however, is inspired.

MAKES 4 LB

3 lb gooseberries, cleaned

1 lb raspberries, cleaned

sugar

Raspberry Juice:

¾ lb raspberries, cleaned

2 cups water

Put the gooseberries and raspberries into a preserving pan with water to cover. Boil for 10 minutes, then strain through a jelly bag for several hours (see page 146) into the cleaned pan.

Meanwhile, make the raspberry juice: Place the raspberries and water in a pan and simmer, covered, for 20 minutes. Strain the juice, discarding the contents of the strainer.

Add the raspberry juice to the pan, and boil briskly for 30 minutes. Measure, and add 1½ cups of sugar to every 2 cups of liquid. Dissolve the sugar over medium heat, then boil for a further 15 minutes or until setting point is reached (see page 145). Pour into warm, sterilized jars, cover, and seal (see page 145). Store in a cool, dark place.

Mulberries In the garden where I spent part of my child-

hood, a spectacular mulberry tree spread its low branches over the small lawn. This heavy

canopy covered the grass, which in summer became encrusted with shining, dark red berries.

As the fruit ripened, pools of staining purple marked the grass. If you picked the fruit, your fin-

gers were immediately marked with a purplish-red dye which was difficult to remove, and woe

betide you if the juice dribbled down your clothing, as it was prone to, since the ripe fruit spurts

its "blood" when you bite into it.

Mulberry Pie *In England, mulberry trees were planted in considerable numbers where the silk*
industry thrived, and it is interesting how many are still found in gardens in and around London. If you are lucky
enough to lay your hands on supplies of this wonderful berry, with its crisp texture and fountains of juice, try making
this fruit pie. It is exceptional. However, if you cannot find mulberries, blackberries make an admirable substitute,
although the flavor will be different.

SERVES 4

2 medium apples, peeled, cored, and sliced

sugar to taste

a pinch of ground cinnamon

1 lb mulberries, cleaned

¼ lb store-bought puff pastry

1 egg, beaten

whipped cream or *Crème Anglaise* (see page 153),
 to serve

Place the apple slices over the bottom of a shallow, buttered pie dish, and sprinkle with a little sugar and a
pinch of cinnamon. Toss the mulberries in some sugar, and spread over the apples.

Roll the dough out to ¼ inch thick and cut it to fit the top of the dish, allowing for a margin of about ⅜ inch.
Moisten the rim of the dish, lay the dough over the top, and press the edges down with a fork. Cut a few
simple flower or petal shapes out of the dough scraps, moisten the undersides, and press them lightly onto the
top as decoration. Brush with the beaten egg. Bake in a preheated oven at 400°F for 10 minutes, then turn the
heat down to 325°F, and bake for a further 10–15 minutes until well risen and golden. Serve hot with whipped
cream or *Crème Anglaise*.

herbs and *Flowers*

An herb garden has its own special beauty. The variety of foliage color, delightful flowers, and above all the fragrances, combine to please the senses, and also do much to attract butterflies and bees throughout summer. Herbs were originally cultivated as "useful plants," for medicinal, culinary, and cosmetic purposes. The herbal tradition is as old as civilization, and the first herb gardens in Europe were planted for monastic infirmaries. Archetypal monastic gardens were little cloisters whose ruins are witness to their past, as are the illustrations in illuminated manuscripts. Such an herb garden might have been walled or hedged around, and placed in a sunny, sheltered position next to the infirmary. Neatly laid out in beds, there would be walkways between the rows of plants to inhale their aromas.

Speak not – whisper not;

Here bloweth thyme and bergamot;

Softly on the evening hour,

Secret herbs their spices shower,

Dark-spiked rosemary and myrrh,

Lean-stalked, purple lavender;

Hides within her bosom, too,

All her sorrows, bitter rue.

A Child's Garden, **Walter de la Mare (1873–1956)**

HERBS AS MEDICINE

Anglo-Saxon herbals list about 500 plants used in medicine and for the recovery of the sick. Our word "drug" comes from the Anglo-Saxon *driggen*, to dry (the herbs). Thus herbs were among the necessities of life, alongside the vegetable patch, vines, and fruits in the orchard, chickens, and bees. Used primarily for healing and flavoring, some herbs also yielded useful dyes for inks and fabrics, others fragrances for incense.

Infirmary herbs included sage, whose generic name comes from the Latin meaning "to be in good health." Traditionally, the first meal given to a monk after sickness and blood-letting was sage and parsley in a dish of soft eggs. "He that would live for aye must eat sage in May," goes an old English proverb. Clary sage was used

as an eyewash, and hyssop as a metabolic stimulant, as well as a strewing herb, loved for its sweet resinous orange scent. Rue found its place in holy water and as an air cleanser, and was found in posies in the English law courts up until the eighteenth century. Chamomile was fondly known as the "plants' physician," a good companion plant which also made a fragrant lawn. Dill was found to soothe the digestive system, and borage to cheer melancholy. All these herbs were used in infusions, or in food, or as strewing herbs to impart their various qualities. Bunches of herbs were gathered at the height of their pungency, and dried in bunches hanging from beams and rafters, to preserve them for the year ahead.

THE COTTAGE GARDEN

Later, as gardening evolved, formal herb gardens came into their own: Herbs lend themselves to garden design because many are hardy, quick growers, and several are evergreen. They also look delightful integrated among border plants, giving an English cottage-garden effect that has echoes from the rural past. The cottager, like the monks, would grow particular herbs with a view to their usefulness for country medicine, for tisanes and cooking, as bee plants, or for all these reasons.

By the sixteenth century the English cottager had his own kitchen garden in addition to an allotment acreage for growing vegetables, and this was to become the woman's domain. Thomas Tusser's *100 Good Points of Husbandry* (1557) recommends dozens of herbs and seeds for kitchen gardens, as well as up to 40 for decoration. He makes clear that both cottager and his wife must "moile and toile" in order to keep a good table and to be prosperous. So he outlines a list of herbs for the kitchen, for teas and tisanes, for salads and sauces, or to boil and butter. He catalogues strewing herbs, herbs and flowers for windowsills and pots, herbs for the still, and medicinal plants, which were also often used as household antiseptics.

Under the umbrella term "herbs" are listed backyard plants, wild flowers, soft fruits, and some vegetables: An "herbe" meant a pungent or aromatic plant that had its place anywhere in the garden or orchard, so the average cottage garden remained a patch where old-fashioned vegetables, fruit, flowers, and herbs mingled in glorious abandon. They were used fresh in spring and summer, and dried for use throughout the winter months.

DECORATIVE HERBS

As garden design became more sophisticated, decorative herb gardens—as distinct from useful ones—came into being: They came into the sights of the rich, the leisured, and the dedicated horticulturist. One common factor remained, however, which was that herbs were still the pastime of the woman of the house: Hers were the medicinal and culinary skills, and literature is strewn with references to women herbalists.

A favorite among garden herbs was the dramatic angelica, tall and stately. Lavender was grown for its inimitable fragrance, as well as being used in cordials, preserves, and lavender water. Lemon balm was, and still is, the classic "bee plant," and makes a wonderful herb tea. Basil, the sweetest of herbs, was used for cooking as well as aromatics, and marjoram and thyme were omnipresent. Mint maintained its reputation from ancient times, in all its varieties and forms, as a cure-all. It was still sometimes called "monks' herb", from its prominence in old infirmary gardens. Savory, cilantro and caraway were found to be good border plants as well as excellent culinary herbs, and used to flavor wine and cakes.

HERB LORE: ROSEMARY

Herbs for the kitchen garden then, as now, included parsley, chervil, lovage, tansy, and—a huge favorite—rosemary. "The perfect herb," it acquired more folklore than any of its peers: For example, that it reaches 33 years of age and never exceeds either Christ's age or his height (the height of a man and a half). Rosemary's reputation acquired a Christian edge: It healed with His compassion, it purified with His grace, and got its mist-blue flowers from the Virgin Mary spreading her cloak over a rosemary bush to dry. A rosemary branch, gilded and tied with silk ribbons, was also presented to wedding guests as a symbol of love and loyalty. Together with an orange stuck with cloves, it was given as a New Year's gift.

The medievals liked to "see the rosmarie in wine ... and thou shalt be merry and lythe." Rosemary tea calmed and "cleansed the body within ... and wash thy visage well therein, it shall make thee whole and clear... For it is kindly ... for it is holy" says a fourteenth century manuscript. Principally, though, rosemary is for remembrance, memorably quoted by Ophelia to Hamlet, and there is an ancient custom of burying the dead with a sprig of rosemary. Sir Thomas More, in a letter to his daughter Margaret, paid his tribute in the sixteenth century: *As for Rosmarie, I lett it runne all over my garden walls, not onlie because my bees love it, but because it is a herb sacred to remembrance, and, therefore, to friendship; whence a sprig of it hath a dumb language that maketh it the chosen emblem of our funeral wakes and in our burial grounds.*

CULINARY HERBS

Cooking with herbs is an extension of the pleasure of herb gardening. Herbs have their place in the greatest of the world's gastronomic dishes. They are distinctive and versatile, a joy to make salads with, as well as to cook with, and they fill the house with their aromas as you work with them in the kitchen.

The flowers of all the herbs mentioned on the following pages, and many wild and garden plants, make elegant edible garnishes, and sometimes flavorings, for summer food. This is a guide to which flowers to use, their colors and flavors. Many are wonderful in salads, some in vinegars, others in ice creams and fruit desserts. They are as much a delight to the palate as a pleasure to the eye. The recipes which follow highlight beautifully the qualities of the herbs used in them.

Marjoram Olives
Closely related to oregano, marjoram was known to the ancient Greeks as "joy of the mountain": Aphrodite, they told, took it from the depths of the ocean to the tops of the highest peaks, where it could grow close to the sun. It is a symbol of peace and happiness.

Indeed, Sir, she was the sweet marjoram of the Salad, or rather the herb of grace.

William Shakespeare

YOU WILL NEED: • **sprigs of marjoram** • **black olives** • **extra-virgin olive oil**

Put the marjoram into a tall jam jar, and add enough olives to come two-thirds of the way up the jar. Fill to cover the olives with olive oil, and shake well. Seal, and store in a cool, dark place.

Leave for several days, or up to several weeks, and the olives will take on the fragrance of the herb. When you have eaten all the olives, decant the oil and use it in salad dressings for tomatoes, beets, or potatoes—all vegetables that can take strong flavors.

Fresh Herb Soup
A summer soup full of the flavors of fresh herbs is one of the delights of the season, evocative of the time when herbs are at their best and most aromatic: May and early June are the months to make the most of these highly aromatic, tender leaves.

SERVES 4

3 tablespoons butter or margarine

¼ cup all-purpose flour

3½ cups Vegetable Stock

2 cups herb leaves, such as lovage, parsley, sage, fennel, thyme, marjoram, balm, etc., chopped

½ lb potatoes, cooked and sliced

salt and freshly ground black pepper

2 tablespoons *crème fraîche* or plain yogurt

herb flowers, to garnish

Melba Toast (see page 155), to serve

Melt the butter or margarine in a large pan, and stir in the flour. Gradually add half the stock, stirring constantly until smooth, and bring to a boil. Add the herb leaves, and simmer gently for 5 minutes. Add the potatoes, simmer for a further 5 minutes and then purée in a blender or food processor. Add the rest of the stock, season to taste, and finally stir in the *crème fraîche* or yogurt. Garnish with a few herb flowers, and serve with Melba Toast.

Gazpacho
This is my personal version of a great Spanish classic: A chilled, uncooked tomato soup. If you grow lovage, use young leaves early in the season for their inimitable flavor; balance this with delicate chervil, and add chives for "bite." These three tastes linger on the palate, and make this herby gazpacho a memorable appetizer for long summer evenings.

SERVES 4

1½ lb tomatoes

1 cup soft fresh bread crumbs

2 cups canned tomato juice

2 canned roasted red peppers, drained and chopped

1 large garlic clove, peeled and finely chopped

3–4 tablespoons olive oil

½ small Spanish onion, very finely chopped

1 small cucumber, peeled and grated

1 tablespoon each finely chopped fresh lovage, chervil, and chives

salt and freshly ground black pepper

2 tablespoons Mayonnaise (see page 122)

To Garnish: chopped black olives and hard-cooked eggs

Croûtons (see page 155)

Peel the tomatoes (see page 102). Chop roughly, and cut out any tough stem. Blend to a smooth purée with the bread crumbs, canned tomato juice, chopped peppers, garlic, and olive oil. Stir in the onion, cucumber, and herbs, and season to taste. Stir in the Mayonnaise to make the soup creamy. Chill thoroughly, and serve with a decorative dish of the garnishes.

Herb Bread
The wonderful aromas of this bread fill the house as it cooks—imagine the smell of fresh yeast dough and fresh herbs drifting out of the oven! It is a perfect bread for simple summer lunches alfresco, to go with the Crème Vichyssoise *on page 78. Good cheeses and fresh fruits of the season would turn it into a feast.*

MAKES A 1½ LB LOAF

2 cups each wholewheat and all-purpose unbleached flour, sifted

1 teaspoon margarine

2 teaspoons each salt and sugar

1 teaspoon dill seed

2 teaspoons chopped fresh savory or marjoram

1 teaspoon chopped fresh dill

½ cake compressed yeast or 2 teaspoons active dry yeast

1 cup warm water

bulgar wheat, for sprinkling the pan

Mix the flours, and rub in the margarine. Add the salt, sugar, dill seed, and herbs, and mix well. Blend the fresh yeast, if using, in the warm water, and when it has dissolved add all at once to the flour mixture. Mix to a soft biscuit-like dough so that it leaves the bowl clean.

If you are using dry yeast, dissolve it in a little of the water with 1 teaspoon of the sugar first, and leave for 10 minutes until frothy. Add with the remaining water to the flour mixture, and again mix well to form the dough.

Knead the dough thoroughly on a lightly floured board. Put into a 2 lb loaf pan, previously greased and sprinkled with bulgar wheat. Place in a warm place, covered with a towel or inside a plastic bag, until the dough doubles in volume, about 2–3 hours. Bake in a preheated oven at 450° for 30–40 minutes. Serve still warm from the oven, with soup, or as a bread and cheese lunch with salad (see Cottage Garden Salad below).

Cottage Garden Salad *Pungent mint is an excellent taste for summer salads, and if lemon balm grows abundantly in your garden, as it does in mine, they complement each other well. Parsley, often overlooked and perceived as ordinary, is nothing of the sort in a salad like this, with its strong, earthy flavor. Choose your own selection from the herb patch, and enjoy the freshness of this garden salad.*

SERVES 2–3

1 crisp head lettuce, washed and shredded

2 baby carrots, scrubbed and diced

1¼ lb red cabbage, washed and finely shredded

¾ cup shelled garden peas, lightly cooked

1 shallot, finely chopped

2 tomatoes, chopped

2 zucchini, thinly sliced and lightly cooked

a handful of alfalfa sprouts

a handful of chopped mixed fresh herbs, such as
   chervil, mint, parsley, and other favorites

1 recipe quantity Vinaigrette (see page 155), made
   with a Flower Vinegar (see page 58), to dress

nasturtium flowers, to decorate

Mix all the salad ingredients together in a big bowl. Dress with the Vinaigrette, and decorate with nasturtium flowers. Serve with Herb Bread (see opposite).

Sallet of ALL KINDS OF HERBS

TO MAKE A SALLET OF ALL KINDS OF HERBS: *Take your Herbs (as the tops of red Sage, Mint, Lettuce, Violets, Marigold, Spinach, etcetera) and pick them very fine in fair water: And wash your flowers by themselves, and swing them in a strainer. Then mingle them in a dish with Cucumbers and Lemons pared and sliced; scrape thereon Sugar and put Vinegar and Oil. Spread your Flowers on top of the Sallet, and take Eggs boiled hard and lay them about the dish.*

A book of Flowers and Fruit, Thomas Jenner, 1653

Summer Salad
Fennel and thyme are two great favorites in my herb garden. Fennel's fine feathery leaves have an aniseedy taste, and are said to impart stamina and strength as well as being good for slimmers. Thyme, so fragrant that it used to be used for incense, still grows on Mount Hymettus as it did in the days of classical Greece, and makes legendary honey: "Homey mistresses and such as keep bees hope to have a good yeare, when they see the Time to bloom abundantly," John Gerard tells us in his Herbal *of 1597. The combined flavors of these two herbs make an unforgettable summer salad.*

SERVES 2–3

1 small head crisp, green lettuce, washed and shredded

1 head red lettuce (oak leaf or *lollo rosso*), washed and dried

1¼ cups small cauliflower florets

2 celery stalks, trimmed and sliced

2 carrots, peeled and cut into matchsticks

6 cherry tomatoes, halved

4 radishes, trimmed and sliced

2 tablespoons each chopped fresh fennel and thyme

1 yellow pepper, seeded and cut into strips

1 small bunch watercress or sweet rocket, washed and dried

1 recipe quantity Vinaigrette (see page 155), made with a Flower Vinegar (see below), to dress

Put the green lettuce into the bottom of a large bowl, and arrange the red leaves around the edge. Place the rest of the salad ingredients, mixed together, into the center. Just before serving, trickle the Vinaigrette over the top, and decorate with flower petals of your choice—stocks petals are among my favorites in high summer.

Herb or Flower VINEGAR
Any of the following give a subtle flavor to vinegars, delightful in salad dressings throughout the summer: Roses, violets, elderflowers, nasturtiums, lavender, rosemary, tarragon, and thyme. You will need one handful of the herb/flower to every 2 cups high-quality white wine vinegar.

Remove the stems, and the green and white "heels" from the flowers and petals, and make sure that the leaves and flowers are clean and perfectly dry. Use wide-necked jars or bottles for the bigger plants.

Place the herb or flowers in a clean bottle or jar, and fill up with the vinegar. Seal, let stand on a sunny windowsill for about 2 weeks, before straining off the vinegar and bottling it.

Right: *Summer salad*

Italian Dip
*This gentle dip has a soft texture and bland, earthy flavors dominated by parsley. Parsley was a symbol of strength to the Greeks and, indeed, it is full of nutritious goodness: Vitamins A, B and C, large amounts of iron and calcium, and many minerals. But there is a proverb from Spanish folklore which warns against eating too much parsley, otherwise you will look older than your years! So balance it in this dip with sweet marjoram, a "settling" herb, which John Gerard (*Herbal, *1597) tells us, "is very good against the warmbling of the stomach."*

SERVES 4

1 medium eggplant

1 medium bunch fresh parsley, chopped

1 medium bunch fresh marjoram, chopped

½ canned roasted red pepper, seeded and chopped

3 tablespoons olive oil

squeeze of lemon juice

salt and freshly ground black pepper

tortilla chips or crudités, to serve

Put the eggplant into boiling water and simmer for 20 minutes, or until completely soft. Cool, then peel. Put the flesh into a blender or food processor with the chopped parsley, marjoram, red pepper, and olive oil. Blend to a dipping consistency. Add a little lemon juice, and season to taste. Serve with tortilla chips or similar spicy snacks, and crudités of your choice.

Pesto Sauce
Pesto is one of the world's best sauces for pasta, and you can also use it to dress tomato salad, or crisp green salad with croûtons. In short, you can improvise endlessly, not only with how to use it, but also with how to make it. The classic pesto is made with basil, garlic, pine nuts, olive oil, and Parmesan cheese. Basil, to the ancients, was the king of herbs, and in India it was made sacred to the god Vishnu. John Gerard tells us in his Herbal *of 1597 that "the smell of Basil is good for the heart... It taketh away sorrowfulness, which cometh of melancholy and maketh a man merry and glad." But there is no reason not to experiment with other nuts and herbs. For example, parsley with walnuts, tarragon with hazelnuts, or dill with almonds. So substitute them accordingly, following this basic method:*

1 large bunch fresh basil, chopped

2 garlic cloves, peeled and crushed

½ cup pine nuts

½ cup olive oil

¼ cup finely grated Parmesan cheese

sea salt

Blend the basil, garlic, and pine nuts with half of the olive oil in a blender or food processor, until smooth. Stir in the rest of the oil and Parmesan, and season with a little sea salt if necessary.

Herb MAYONNAISE

Add 2 tablespoons very finely chopped fresh tarragon to the Mayonnaise on page 122, and let stand
for at least 2 hours before serving. Other herbs which make excellent Herb Mayonnaise are:

• chives

• parsley

• marjoram

• basil

• cilantro

• savory—or a judicious mixture of *fines herbes*—according to taste.

Flower Ice Cream *Flowers were used far more frequently in the old days than they are today,*
yet they are wonderful both for flavor and to decorate dishes. This ice cream is simply amazing, a scented, delicate, and
creamy dessert which makes an elegant end to a summer's day. The best petals to use are undoubtedly well-scented roses,
or stocks and honeysuckle: Your senses will reel!

SERVES 4

1 cup heavy cream

½ cup scented petals

½ teaspoon orange-flower water

2 eggs, separated

¾ cup sugar

extra petals, to decorate

Heat the cream gently, and stir in the petals. Let stand over a pan of hot water (not boiling) for 10–15 minutes
to allow the petals to infuse. Keep it covered. Then allow to cool completely before adding the orange-flower
water. Strain.

Beat the cream until thick. Beat the egg yolks with the sugar until thick and pale yellow, and then fold in
the cream. Beat the egg whites until very stiff, and fold them in. Put into a freezer container, cover, and freeze
for 1 hour. Remove from the freezer, blend until smooth, then cover and return to the freezer for the final
freezing. Alternatively, use an ice-cream maker, and follow the manufacturer's instructions.

Serve in scoops, slightly softened, and decorate each helping with fresh petals.

the vegetable *Patch*

Then a sentimental passion of vegetable fashion must excite your languid spleen,

An attachment à la Plato for a bashful young potato, or a not too French French bean!

Though the Philistines may jostle, you will rank as an apostle in the high aesthetic band,

If you walk down Piccadilly with a poppy or a lily in your medieval hand.

And everyone will say,

As you walk your flowery way,

"If he's content with a vegetable love which would certainly not suit me,

Why, what a most particularly pure young man this pure young man must be!"

Patience, W. S. Gilbert, 1881

The basic vegetables of medieval Europe were indeed basic. A twelfth-century English treatise gives a clue: "In a kitchen there should be a small table on which cabbage may be minced, and also lentils, peas, shelled beans, beans in the pod, millet, onions and other vegetables of the kind that can be cut up." The fact is that the medieval palate was not highly tuned to the delicacy of vegetables as we know them today: They liked them to be either starchy or strong in flavor, and always as a small supplement to a diet largely carnivorous, backed up by bread, cheese and ale. This humble culinary tradition reflected the lifestyle of the majority: A simple rural economy prevailed, based on a two-tiered class system, untouched in those early days by the demands of fashion that are so imperative today.

In England, the cottager, who represented the majority of the population, had a little "patch" rather than

a garden, in which fruit trees, vegetables, herbs, and flowers all grew together, well manured by the resident livestock, household slops and privy, vegetable refuse and chimney soot. Chickens scratched around, maybe there was a beehive, perhaps geese and ducks as well, and some cottagers kept a pig. Field strips allowed the householder to supplement his food supply and kept him in enough peas and beans to see him through the winter. The bean, especially, was ubiquitous because of its food value, and a symbol of necessary wealth: The English saying, "I haven't got a bean," grew out of a medieval proverb. Edward Lear exercised his limerick skills on this humble subject:

There was an old person of Dean
Who dined on one pea and one bean;
For he said, "More than that
Would make me too fat."
That cautious old person of Dean.

Book of Nonsense, Edward Lear, 1846

The Anglo-Saxon word for a gardener was a "leek-ward," indicating their preference for strong tastes, which also accounts for their use of pungent herbs, both cultivated and wild. Chaucer's Summoner in *The Canterbury Tales* (*c.*1387) "well loved ... garlic onions and eke [moreover] leeks." The leek was the winter vegetable or pot-herb *par excellence*, and the *Allium* family in general became the stock-in-trade of English peasant cookery. Records of 1333 from Glastonbury Abbey show that they produced 5,000 cloves of garlic that year. Garlic sauce with goose on Sundays was a traditional feast for those who had the resources.

But, overall, the medieval countryman didn't bother much with vegetables. They were used mainly in soup, and for boiling up with meat in the "pot", especially with bacon. Even on the tables of the rich they made relatively rare appearances. Vegetables and herbs were used on fasting days in the monasteries, and cabbage was ubiquitous. Generally it was cooked from dawn until dusk, almost to a purée, then heavily spiced with salt, mustard, garlic, or vinegar. The name "cabbage" comes from the medieval "caboche," derived from the Latin *caput*, head. By the fifteenth century the bourgeois classes were treating cabbages as individual vegetables, and served them buttered, although the smartest and most affluent ate cabbage as a salad vegetable.

Vegetables are to some extent a social barometer; they tell quite a lot about aspects of living at any given period among different social groups. As trade and travel began to open up Europe in the sixteenth century, so accordingly, did the appearance of vegetables on the table. By the mid-sixteenth century, Thomas Tusser, in his *100 Good Points of Husbandry* of 1557, lists asparagus, beans, beets, cabbage, carrots, cucumber, globe artichokes, gourds, leeks, onions, parsnips, peas, pumpkin, radishes, skirret, spinach, and turnips. There was no mention yet of potatoes and tomatoes, which did not arrive on the scene until the end of the century.

A quarter of an acre was long thought to be a suitable size plot on which a man could cultivate enough to feed his family well, and by the seventeenth century the list had expanded to include Windsor beans, scarlet runners, early potatoes, Prussian Potatoes, Devonshire potatoes, radishes, Cos lettuce, barley, and tobacco! Families would supplement their diet with wild vegetables and herbs, such as hop-tops, fat hen, nettles, and sorrel, and the canny would plant sloe for hedging, so that they could make sloe gin in the fall for winter consumption. High hedges of crab apple of great antiquity can still be seen in parts of England, planted for a similar dual purpose: The hedge supplied the larder shelf.

By the eighteenth century, once the potato had become established in Britain, it became a delicacy for the rich man's table, often cooked with spices or even candied. Onions and artichokes had been mentioned by John Parkinson in his *Paradisi in Sole* of 1620, along with the regular medieval pot herbs, including turnips, described as "a poor man's feast, very windy." A century later, stately grounds would include a walled vegetable garden with gravel paths and rustic arch, and the gardener grew mushrooms and asparagus alongside melons, vines, and strawberries. But for poorer folk things stayed much the same: In *Our Village*, written in the 1820s, Miss Mitford mentions all the fruits, but doesn't deem vegetables worthy of mention. It was taken as read that onions, leeks, root vegetables, cabbage, peas, carrots, and salad vegetables were grown, but these were too ordinary to be noteworthy. Yet Gilbert White, author of *The Natural History of Selbourne*, 1789, attributed the decline of leprosy in Britain to a general increase in the eating of vegetables! However, although Wordsworth sowed scarlet runner beans in his garden, it is said that his favorite place to be was in the orchard.

By Wordsworth's time, allotment gardens were beginning to catch on. Even though England's first Act of Parliament had been passed in 1819, the idea had not enjoyed instant success, since the concept of a strip of land, not attached to a house, of about a quarter of an acre, for those who could afford the rent, did not have popular appeal. It took time to engage into the social fabric of Britain, but, once established, it became a popular and socially important phenomenon, which persists into modern life.

The second half of the twentieth century has seen an ever-increasing interest in vegetables, and a marked change in their cooking and usage. Vegetables came to be respected in their own right, often cooked with enticing flavorings and spices, influenced by ethnic cultures from around the world. As ever a gauge of social and cultural change, the expansion of worldwide food markets has led to the appearance of exotic vegetables from all corners of the globe on the supermarket shelf. Whereas, in the 1950s, the greengrocer would boast little more than Tusser's catalogue for its regular produce, today the display is wide-ranging, bright, and intriguing. A rise in vegetarianism has embraced this development, and the two have been mutually supportive: Vegetarian cooking came out of its brown-rice-and-sandals image into a world of inspired and creative cuisine, motivated not least by a growing concern among the public for a healthy diet. This makes it all the more satisfying to grow your own fresh vegetables for using all year round. The flavor of newly gathered garden produce is incomparably better than commercially produced vegetables, and a well-planned vegetable patch can keep you in food throughout the year.

Potatoes

The potato was discovered in the New World by the Conquistadores, and grown in botanical gardens in Spain, although to start with not many people were interested in eating them. The Irish were the first Europeans to consume them on a large scale. Not until the nineteenth century did England and Scotland start to cultivate them widely, followed by France.

These potatoes be the most delicate rootes that may be eaten, and doe farre exceed our parseneps or carets. Their pines be of the bignes of two fists, the outside whereof is of the making of a pine-apple, but it is soft like the rinde of a Cucumber, and the inside eateth like an apple but it is more delicious than any sweet apple sugred.

Sir Francis Drake, late sixteenth century

Colcannon

By the end of the seventeenth century potatoes were the most important food crop in Ireland. Colcannon is a typically Irish way of cooking them.

SERVES 4

1½ lb potatoes, peeled and boiled until tender

8 scallions, trimmed and sliced

½ cup hot milk

½ stick butter or margarine

¾ lb outer cabbage leaves, shredded and cooked

salt and freshly ground black pepper

Drain the potatoes, and dry them quickly over gentle heat, tossing in the pan. Set to one side. Pour boiling water over the scallions in a bowl to soften them. Drain, and heat them gently with the milk for 5–6 minutes. Mash the potatoes, and beat the milk mixture in until soft and light.

Melt the butter or margarine in a pan, and toss the shredded cabbage in it. Fold into the potato. Season generously. You can serve it as it is, or sauté it in butter, oil, or dripping like a thick pancake, until the outside is crusty, crisp, and brown (see Fried Potato Cake on page 68).

Potato SALAD

There are endless variations on the theme of potato salad. It is best to use waxy, young potatoes—the floury ones do not make good salads. Slice, season, and dress them while still warm. Improvisation is the name of the game:

- with chopped raw onions in mayonnaise
- in vinaigrette, with chopped chives
- with strips of grilled bell pepper and green olives, in mayonnaise
- with celery and fresh herbs, having sprinkled some white wine over the potatoes while still warm. Dress with a light mayonnaise
- with artichoke hearts and salsify and rosemary, in mayonnaise

Fried Potato Cake
Potatoes are always substantial and nourishing, and this fried potato cake, or hash, conjures memories of childhood for me, supper food on bleak winter evenings.

YOU WILL NEED: • meat dripping or oil • leftover cooked potatoes, roughly mashed

Melt some meat dripping or oil in a deep, thick-bottomed skillet. When it is smoking, press in the potatoes. Turn the heat down a little. As the bottom browns, keep stirring it from the bottom until the mass is full of fried brown pieces. Then press it all down firmly, and let cook over gentle heat for 10–15 minutes until the bottom is evenly browned and crusty. Invert onto a platter to serve.

P a r s n i p s
The parsnip is cultivated throughout the northern hemisphere. Parsnip tops have been fed to pigs and cattle for centuries: "In October, the leaves of the parsnips should be given to cows... They will impart much richness to the milk," says Lawson's *Agricultural Manual* of 1858. They have, therefore, invited ridicule from those who are not enamored of them, although parsnips are a versatile and delicate vegetable. Their sweet flavor was extremely popular in medieval times, plus the useful fact that they could stay in the ground over winter. Parsnips are best eaten after the first frost, since then the flavor becomes more mellow.

Parsnip Fries
Parsnips are perhaps best loved in English cookery roasted alongside potatoes with the Sunday roast. Here is another popular way of cooking them, just like French fries. They melt in the mouth.

YOU WILL NEED: • **parsnips** • **oil for deep-frying**

Wash and scrape sufficient parsnips for your meal, and cut each into four wedges. Keep dividing these wedges until you have pieces about the thickness of a pencil. Put into enough cold water to cover, and bring to a boil. Cook for 2–3 minutes. Drain, and dry on a clean cloth.

Heat the oil in a deep pan or deep-fat fryer until smoking, and cook the fries until crisp and golden. Drain on absorbent paper towels, and pile high onto a hot platter. These, with baked fall tomatoes and thick, crusty bread, make a country supper in themselves.

Curried Parsnip Soup
Parsnips make a wonderful, warming, winter soup, especially when spiced with hot curry flavors, which are an excellent foil to the sweetness of the vegetable. This soup makes a satisfying lunch served with warm wholewheat bread and butter.

SERVES 3–4

1 medium onion, peeled and chopped

1 large parsnip, peeled and chopped

2 tablespoons butter or margarine

1 tablespoon flour

½ teaspoon curry powder

4 cups Vegetable Stock

½ cup heavy cream (optional)

1 tablespoon chopped fresh parsley

salt and freshly ground black pepper

Croûtons (see page 155), to serve

Cook the chopped onion and parsnip gently in the butter or margarine, covered, for 10 minutes, stirring so that they do not brown but become soft and sweet. Stir in the flour and curry powder to taste. Cook for 2 minutes, stirring, then pour in the stock gradually. Simmer until the parsnips are tender, 5–8 minutes more. Blend to a fine purée in a blender or food processor. Add more stock if necessary, or cream, if you prefer. Stir in the chopped fresh parsley. Heat through, but do not let boil, and adjust the seasoning. Serve the soup with Croûtons.

$\mathcal{T}urnips$ There is an English saying, "not worth a withered neep," which describes the generally low opinion of the humble turnip: You have to be hungry to bother with it. But the further north in England you go, the more popular, it seems, does this earth-flavored root become. Turnips are best eaten young, before their flavor becomes too strong.

Glazed Turnips *Young turnips, lightly cooked so that they are still crisp, then sautéed in butter with a little sugar, make a delectable side dish to go with roast chicken or game birds.*

SERVES 2

1 lb young turnips, peeled and cut into
   ¾ inch dice

salt

a generous pat of butter

2 tablespoons sugar

Blanch the turnips in boiling salted water until cooked but still slightly crisp. Drain. Melt the butter in a heavy-bottomed pan, and put the turnips in. Sprinkle with the sugar. Sauté briskly until the turnips caramelize to a golden color. Keep stirring so as not to burn the sugar. Serve hot.

Lancashire Turnips and Carrots *This rough "mash" of carrots and turnips is very English, very traditional, and substantial food.*

SERVES 4

1 lb turnips, peeled or scrubbed, and roughly
   chopped

1 lb carrots, peeled or scrubbed, and roughly
   chopped

2 tablespoons butter or margarine

2 tablespoons flour

salt and freshly ground black pepper

slice of hot, buttered toast or crisp salad, to serve

Cook the turnips and carrots together in boiling water until soft. Drain, reserving the cooking liquid. Make a sauce by melting the butter or margarine over low heat, stirring in the flour, and gradually adding the cooking liquid, stirring all the time. Season, and simmer gently until the sauce thickens, about 6–8 minutes.

Mash the vegetables roughly, season, and put them into a hot ovenproof dish. Pour the hot sauce over the top and fold into the vegetables. Bake at 350°F for 25 minutes until bubbling. Serve with buttered toast or crisp salad.

Jerusalem Artichokes

"Jerusalem" artichokes is a misnomer: They have nothing to do with the Holy Land. "Jerusalem" is a corruption of *girasole*, or sunflower. It is a stately, sculptural plant, ideal for siting along the edge of a vegetable garden. The taste, however, is reminiscent of artichoke.

Palestine Soup

A winter soup made with Jerusalem artichokes is a treat to look forward to as the cold weather arrives. Serve with warm seeded rolls.

SERVES 4

2 lb Jerusalem artichokes, washed and chopped

1 onion, peeled and chopped

2 tablespoons butter

salt and freshly ground black pepper

2 cups milk

2 cups Vegetable Stock

2 tablespoons light cream

Croûtons (see page 155), to serve

Place the artichokes and onion in a pan, cover with water, and simmer until soft. Drain. Rub through a fine strainer, or purée in a blender or food processor. Stir in the butter, season well with salt and pepper, and mix in the milk and stock. Heat through and it is ready to serve. Swirl in the cream just before serving, and pass Croûtons to sprinkle over the top.

Artichoke Fritters

These fritters are irresistible – wonderfully crisp on the outside, and runny inside. Serve as an appetizer, sprinkled with parsley and a little sea salt.

SERVES 3–4

1 lb Jerusalem artichokes, washed

flour

salt and freshly ground black pepper

1 recipe quantity Fritter Batter (see page 154)

vegetable oil for deep-frying

Parboil the artichokes in their skins for 10 minutes, or until tender but not mushy. Drain, and peel them when cooled. Slice them. Drop into well-seasoned flour, then coat in the batter. Deep-fry in very hot oil until crisp and golden all over. Drain on absorbent paper towels, and serve at once.

Artichoke and Leek Hot-Pot

A young English botanist, John Goodyear, writing in the early seventeenth century, was of the opinion that "which way soever they be dressed and eaten they still cause a filthy loathsome stinking wind, thereby causing the belly to be pained and tormented." But don't let him put you off: The artichoke—although admittedly windy—is a gastronomic vegetable, a delicacy, as this simple hot-pot illustrates. It tastes of the country—truly rural food—and is delicious served with crusty or wholewheat bread, as a light meal on its own, or as a side dish to accompany fish or meat.

SERVES 2–3

1 lb Jerusalem artichokes, peeled and halved

2 medium leeks, washed, trimmed, and cut into
  1 inch lengths

salt and freshly ground black pepper

curry powder to taste

3 cups Vegetable Stock (see page 154)

2 tablespoons chopped fresh parsley

Pack the artichokes and leeks into a large casserole dish, seasoning a little as you go with salt, pepper, and curry powder. Barely cover with stock. Cover with a lid, and simmer very gently for about 12–15 minutes, until the vegetables are tender. Strain off the stock, season with more salt, pepper, and curry powder, if necessary, and serve sprinkled with the chopped parsley.

*B*eets

Beets were developed by German gardeners in the Middle Ages, and it is a superb vegetable. Freshly dug baby beets are matchless—the smell of them while boiling is incomparable.

Beet Gratin

An old English cookbook describes how beets "make a colorful dish of 'plain cooked vegetables' from the allotment," and although this is true, it is also to underrate it. Beets make a wonderful dish in their own right, as this gratin demonstrates.

SERVES 3–4

6 medium beets, boiled and peeled

2 tablespoons grated Parmesan cheese

2 tablespoons grated Cheddar cheese

salt and freshly ground black pepper

5 tablespoons light cream

bread crumbs

a little butter or margarine

Cut the beets into small dice. Sprinkle one-third of the cheeses over the bottom of a small gratin dish, and put half the beets on top, packed down tightly. Season, then repeat the layers, ending with a layer of cheese. Pour in enough cream just to cover, and scatter bread crumbs over the top. Dot with butter or margarine. Bake in a preheated oven for 15 minutes at 375°F.

Borsch *The most famous dish of the Russian culinary canon, borsch is indeed a major treat. Its rich color and earthy flavors make it excellent warming winter food, yet borsch is also delicious served chilled, and always with that dollop of sour cream in the center.*

SERVES 4–6

1 lb raw beets

1 small head white cabbage, quartered

4 cups Vegetable Stock (see page 154)

2 tablespoons vinegar

2 potatoes, peeled and diced

salt and freshly ground black pepper

lemon juice to taste

sugar to taste

⅓ cup sour cream

Peel the raw beets, and grate them coarsely. Blanch the white cabbage in boiling water for 3–4 minutes, then shred it finely. Put the cabbage into a large saucepan, and simmer in the stock until tender. In a separate pan, cook the grated beets in water with the vinegar until tender, about 10 minutes, then add, with the cooking liquid, to the cooked cabbage and stock. Add the diced potatoes, and season with salt and pepper. Add lemon juice and sugar to taste. Simmer for a further 25 minutes, or just until the flavors are well amalgamated. Purée in a blender or food processor, adjust the seasoning, and serve with a bowl of the sour cream to pass separately.

Beets as a SIDE VEGETABLE

• Boil beets in their skin: Wash, then cook in boiling water until tender, and peel when cool enough to handle. The cooking time depends on the size of the beets.

• Roasted beets are delicious. Wash and peel, then cut into chunks, and drizzle with oil. Bake at 375°F for 40–45 minutes, or until tender, turning often. Serve with freshly ground black pepper .

• Sliced boiled beets are lovely with spinach, served in layers with a garnish of Croûtons (see page 155).

Carrots

Carrots have been around for a long time. They were known to the Roman epicure Apicius, who gave recipes for fried carrots and carrots with parsnips. Later, gardeners developed four main varieties: Purple, yellow, white, and orange. Nor was the root the only part used: In the time of Charles I, ladies at Court wore carrot foliage in their hats!

Spiced Carrot Soup

This richly orange-colored soup is a favorite standby for long periods of the year. It is thick and satisfying, the spiciness pleasing to the palate—and of course it is teeming with vitamin A!

SERVES 2–3

1 lb carrots, peeled or scrubbed

1–2 teaspoons curry powder

2 cups Vegetable Stock (see page 154)

heavy cream or yogurt to taste

sea salt

thin toast or pita bread, to serve

Simmer the carrots in a pan of water until very well cooked. Blend to a purée with the curry powder and stock in a blender or food processor. Thin out to the desired consistency, if necessary, with a little water, and add some cream or yogurt to taste. Heat through, but do not boil. Season to taste with a little sea salt, and serve immediately with thin toast or pita bread.

Glazed Carrots

In medieval times vegetables were called "wortes," and usually boiled to death with a flank of fairly tough meat. How times have changed: These glazed carrots have subtlety and a light touch.

SERVES 3–4

¾ lb carrots, peeled or scrubbed

1 tablespoon butter or margarine

2 tablespoons sugar

salt

Slice the carrots diagonally. Cover with water in a saucepan, add the butter or margarine, sugar, and a pinch of salt. Boil steadily until almost cooked, then turn up the heat to cook vigorously, in order to reduce the liquid down to a shiny glaze. Be careful not to overdo it or else the glaze will caramelize.

Left: *Glazed carrots*

Gratin of Carrots *This completely unpretentious dish is delicate and satisfying, and an appetizing contrast of creamy and crisp textures.*

SERVES 3–4

1 lb carrots, peeled or scrubbed,
   thickly sliced, and cooked

1 recipe quantity Béchamel Sauce (see
   page 154)

2 tablespoons light cream

salt and freshly ground black pepper

⅓ cup grated cheese

⅓ cup fine dry bread crumbs

melted butter or margarine

Put the cooked carrots into the Béchamel Sauce, and stir in the cream. Season to taste, then put in an oven-proof dish. Top with the grated cheese mixed with the bread crumbs. Dribble a little melted butter or margarine over the top, and brown in a preheated oven at 375° for 10 minutes.

Best Carrot Cake *"Sowe Carrets in your Gardens, and humbly praise God for them, as for a singular and great blessing," says Richard Gardiner in his* Profitable Instructions for the Manuring, Sowing and Planting of Kitchen Gardens *of 1599. A blessing indeed: Where would we be without carrot cake? This one is brilliant, the best recipe I know. It freezes well.*

SERVES 6

1 stick margarine

¾ cup sugar

3 eggs

2 cups flour

1 teaspoon baking soda

2 teaspoons cinnamon

1 lb carrots, peeled or scrubbed, and finely grated

½ cup raisins or golden raisins

⅓ cup chopped nuts, such as walnuts or pecans
   (optional)

Cream the margarine with the sugar, then beat in the eggs alternately with half the flour, sifted with the baking soda and cinnamon. Stir in the carrots, and fold in the rest of the flour. Finally, stir in the raisins or golden raisins, and the nuts, if using. Place in a greased 8-inch cake pan and bake in a preheated oven at 350°F for 40–45 minutes, until just set—it should still be a little moist in the center; the cooking time varies according to the water content of the carrots. Cool a little in the pan, then invert onto a wire rack, and leave until cold.

Celeriac Although this vegetable has long been a part of the European culinary tradition, it is only just coming into its own and making its mark farther afield. It has a beautiful flavor, and is a valuable and interesting winter vegetable. It discolors when cut, so dip it into acidulated water (2 tablespoons lemon juice or 1 tablespoon vinegar, to 4 cups water).

Celeriac Rémoulade *This salad, best served as an hors d'oeuvre, is of French inspiration.*

SERVES 4

1 medium celeriac root, peeled

1 recipe quantity Mayonnaise (see page 122)

1–2 tablespoons Dijon mustard, to taste

chopped fresh parsley, to garnish

Cut the peeled celeriac into fine julienne strips. Mix the Mayonnaise with the mustard, check for flavor, and then mix thoroughly with the celeriac. Garnish with chopped parsley.

Celeriac Gratin *Slices of cooked celeriac in cheese or tomato sauce, topped with a crust of bread crumbs and cheese, make a delightful side dish or a perfect meal for vegetarians, served with crusty bread and a winter salad.*

SERVES 2–3

1 medium celeriac root, peeled

¼ cup Parmesan cheese, grated

2-3 tablespoons butter or margarine

Béchamel Sauce (see page 154) or Fresh Tomato
  Sauce (see page 102)

⅓ cup Cheddar cheese, grated

1 cup fresh bread crumbs

Cut the celeriac into slices, and cook in boiling water until tender. Arrange in a buttered gratin dish, scattering each layer with the grated Parmesan and pats of butter or margarine. Cover with the sauce of your choice. Mix the grated Cheddar with the bread crumbs, and sprinkle over the top. Dot with little pieces of the remaining butter or margarine, and bake in a preheated oven at 350°F for 20 minutes, until nicely browned.

ℒeeks

In England, the strong Welsh connection with the leek is its primary association for many people. In AD 640, the Welsh fought a successful battle against the Saxons, and according to legend stuck leeks in their hats to distinguish themselves from the enemy.

Leeks disappeared from the tables of the gentry in the sixteenth and seventeenth centuries, and have only relatively recently made their return to popularity in Britain. Leeks are best eaten fairly young, before they grow too thick, and they don't improve with long cooking.

Crème Vichyssoise

In spite of its French name, this is an American soup, invented in New York and first served at the Ritz Carlton in 1917. It is stunning: An unforgettable pale green color, with delicate, fine flavors. Serve chilled, sprinkled with chives.

SERVES 4–6

6 leeks, washed, trimmed, and finely sliced

½ stick unsalted butter

5 medium potatoes, peeled and finely sliced

5 cups Vegetable Stock (see page 154)

salt

¾ cup heavy cream or *crème fraîche*

chopped fresh chives, to garnish

Soften the leeks in the butter over gentle heat for 5–6 minutes. Add the potatoes, and cook for a further 5 minutes, stirring. Add the stock and salt to taste, and simmer gently for 30–40 minutes, covered. Purée in a blender or food processor until very smooth. Cool.

When the soup is cold, stir in the cream or *crème fraîche*, and then chill thoroughly. Serve sprinkled with chopped fresh chives.

Leekie Pie

Dorothy Hartley writes of leeks in Food in England, *"it is a mistake to serve these delicate vegetables with thick sauce; the liquor and butter together in the dish should be sufficient." She is right; braised in milk and/or butter until just tender, they are superb, either as a side dish or as here, in an old-fashioned pie.*

SERVES 4

1½ recipe quantities Shortcrust Dough (see page 150)

2½ lb young leeks, washed, trimmed, and thinly
   sliced

3 tablespoons butter or margarine

salt and freshly ground black pepper

Roll out two-thirds of the dough, and use to line a greased deep 9-inch pie dish. Soften the leeks slightly by sweating them in the butter or margarine, in a covered pan, for 10 minutes, stirring occasionally. Pack them into the pie dish, and season with salt and pepper. Roll out the remaining dough to form a lid, and use to cover the pie. Seal the edges well. Make a slit in the top of the pie. Bake in a preheated oven at 375°F for 40–50 minutes, until the crust is a fine crisp brown. Serve hot or warm.

Flamiche

The Victorians decreed that leeks "tainted the breath," and deemed them peasant food. But leeks are a fine winter vegetable, which lend themselves to gastronomic dishes. This flamiche, or open tart, is a fine example of peasant food of distinction.

SERVES 3–4

Dough:

1¼ cups all-purpose flour, plus extra for kneading

3 tablespoons butter or margarine, cut into small

    pieces

salt

1 package active dry yeast, dissolved in

    2 tablespoons warm water

1 egg, beaten

Filling:

3 lb leeks, washed

½ stick butter or margarine

3 egg yolks

½ cup *crème fraîche* or yogurt

salt and freshly ground black pepper

To make the dough, sift the flour, and rub in the pieces of butter or margarine. Add a pinch of salt. Make a well in the center, and put in the yeast mixture and beaten egg. Mix, and knead until smooth. Add a little water if necessary. Roll into a ball, and make a cross-cut on the top. Place in a bowl, and leave in a warm place, covered with a cloth, to rise for 2 hours.

About 30 minutes before the dough is ready, start to prepare the filling. Chop the white part of the leeks (reserving the green part for soup or stock), and stew in the butter or margarine until cooked to a pulp.

When the dough is ready, sprinkle with flour and punch it down. Knead, and press into an 8-inch tart pan with your knuckles. Spread the leeks on top. Beat the egg yolks with the *crème fraîche* (or yogurt), and season with salt and pepper. Pour over the leeks. Bake at 400°F for 20 minutes, then at 350°F for a further 20 minutes. Serve hot or warm.

Onions

The onion, chief of the Allium *family of which garlic, too, is a member, is older than recorded history. So venerated was it in ancient Egypt that the priests forbade the people to eat it. An onion was placed in the hands of mummies to help their journey to the underworld, as it would ward off evil and give them protection.*

Tarte à l'Oignon

This tart is country cooking at its best: Simple, and with that sublimely sweet flavor of melted onions.

SERVES 6–8

1 recipe quantity Shortcrust Dough (see page 150)

1½ lb onions, peeled and thinly sliced

3 tablespoons butter or margarine

2 eggs, beaten

½ cup grated Gruyère cheese

salt, freshly ground black pepper, and ground nutmeg

Roll out the dough, and use to line a greased 9-inch tart. Stew the onions in the butter or margarine for 30 minutes, with the pan covered, stirring occasionally and making sure that they don't brown. Remove from the heat and stir in the beaten eggs. Fold in the grated Gruyère. Season with salt, pepper, and nutmeg. Pour into the tart shell, and bake at 350°F for 20–30 minutes, until set. Serve warm or cold.

Pickled ONIONS

Bread-and-cheese-and-pickled-onions was traditional English country food for centuries, carried in a bag or pocket to the fields for the noonday meal. Pickled onions were made in vast quantities by rural folk, using small onions especially grown for the purpose.

Pick the largest of the onions off the top of the stalk. Peel them, and put into 10 per cent Brine (see page 149) for 3 days. Remove and drain them, then rinse, and pack into cold, sterilized jars. Pour cold Spiced Vinegar (see page 149) over them. Cover and seal, then leave for 6 months before using.

To make decorative jars for presents, arrange the onions in the jars with red chilies and green capers. You can also tint the vinegar golden by boiling the papery outer skins of onion in it.

Right: *Pickled onions*

Scallion TANSY

The "tansy" is a cross between scrambled eggs and an omelet, cooked with onion tops or scallions. A delightful, simple dish for a light supper, served with new potatoes and tossed salad. I can't improve on the wording of this old country recipe:

Take holsters [bolted onions] in spring, chop them finely and fry in bacon fat. When they are soft drain off any fat, and pour on enough beaten egg to cover, and pepper and salt to chase them around—until blended— and then "leave 'em be" till set, "not let them boil, mind, or the egg will be all a whey, just set it nicely." Turn on to a hot plate, and it is excellent.

I made this recipe for two people using 3 scallions, 3 eggs, and 1 tablespoon margarine. We ate it for lunch with fresh wholewheat bread and tossed salad, and it was a feast.

S o u b i s e   *Soubise is a purée of onions, which have been cooked very slowly and gently until they are soft and sweet and have lost their pungency, a technique which is the basis of* soupe à l'oignon gratinée, *one of France's great peasant dishes. Soubise is a delectable sauce, wonderful with chicken and new potatoes, or over soft-cooked eggs.*

MAKES 1½ CUPS

½ lb onions, peeled and very thinly sliced

3 tablespoons butter or margarine

1 tablespoon flour, sifted

salt, freshly ground black pepper, and
  ground nutmeg

½ cup warm milk or stock

light cream (optional)

Soften the sliced onions in butter or margarine in a pan over gentle heat, covered with a lid, for about 12–15 minutes, until pale yellow in color but not browned. Stir from time to time. When they have all but melted, stir in the flour, and season to taste with salt, pepper, and a little nutmeg. Add the milk or stock, and simmer very gently for 15 minutes.

Strain or blend so that the sauce is quite smooth. Thin out, if necessary, with light cream, and check the seasoning.

Onionskin EGGS

Cut the outer skin carefully from larger onions, and wrap it around eggs with a wet cloth. Tie securely. Boil the eggs until they are hard. Cool in cold water, then remove the cloth and onion skin, and dry. You can then polish them with grease and you will have a beautifully shiny, mottled, striped or marbled, golden-brown egg.

Celery

Celery never played much of a role in English cookery until after the 1880s. It has to be blanched up, that is, grown in trenches, but you are well rewarded if you do grow your own—both taste and texture are a revelation.

Celery and Cheese Soup

Do use the leaves as well as the stalks when you are making celery soup—they add immensely to the flavor. This soup is inimitable, served on a very cold day for lunch with crusty bread and butter. If you like blue cheese, you can try making it with Danish Blue or Stilton.

SERVES 4

1 medium head of celery, trimmed and chopped

2 medium onions, peeled and chopped

½ stick butter or margarine

¼ cup all-purpose flour

4 cups Vegetable Stock (see page 154)

½ cup grated Gruyère or Cheddar cheese

salt and freshly ground black pepper

2 tablespoons chopped fresh parsley or dill

triangles of fried bread or fingers of toast, to serve

Cook the chopped vegetables in the butter or margarine over gentle heat, covered, for 10 minutes until soft but not brown. Stir in the flour, then add the stock slowly, stirring until the mixture becomes smooth and thick. Cover, and simmer for 40 minutes, until the celery is very tender.

Purée in a blender or food processor. Return to the heat, and add the grated cheese. Heat gently until the cheese melts. Check the seasoning, and stir in the herbs. Serve with triangles of fried bread, or fingers of toast.

Winter SALADS

John Evelyn, the eighteenth century diarist, called celery "the grace of the whole board," meaning when served with cheese, and how right he was. Fresh, crisp, raw celery is one of winter's best things, and perfect in salads. Use the "hearts," too, for their unique flavor and texture. Here are a few salad ideas:

• chopped celery with Jerusalem artichokes (chopped raw), and mustard-and-cress seedlings

• Waldorf salad: Chopped celery, chopped apple, and chopped walnuts in mayonnaise

• chopped celery, chopped apple, and cubes of Gruyère cheese in mayonnaise

• celery, tomatoes, beets, and chopped hazelnuts in mayonnaise

• chopped celery, potatoes, and beets in mayonnaise

*A*sparagus *I revere the memory of Mr F as an estimable man and most indulgent husband, only necessary to mention Asparagus and it appears ... it was not ecstasy but it was comfort.*

Flora Finching in *Little Dorrit*, Charles Dickens, 1857

Asparagus Soup *An elegant and delicate summer soup, you can serve this either hot, with Croûtons (see page 155), or chilled with Melba Toast (see page 155). It is one of the delights of high summer.*

SERVES 4

24 medium asparagus stalks, washed and woody part
  of stems removed

1 shallot, peeled and finely chopped

3 cups Vegetable Stock (see page 154)

salt and freshly ground black pepper

2 tablespoons butter

¼ cup flour

1 cup heavy cream

Cut the asparagus stems into 1-inch lengths, saving eight tips for garnish. Simmer the shallot with the asparagus in the stock, covered, for about 20 minutes. Meanwhile, steam the reserved tips until just tender, and keep warm on one side.

Process the stock with the cooked shallot and asparagus in a blender or food processor until smooth, and pass through a strainer, if necessary, if there are stringy bits still in the purée. Heat through, and season to taste.

Work the butter and flour to a smooth paste, divide into small pieces and whisk, off the heat, into the soup. Heat gently, stirring constantly, until thickened and well blended. Serve hot or chilled. Swirl the cream into each portion as you serve, adding two of the reserved tips to each bowl.

To steam ASPARAGUS

Trim the woody ends off the asparagus stems, wash, then sort into bundles of even size, and tie up with string. Cook them upright in a tall saucepan so that only the thick stems stand in boiling water, and the delicate heads are just steamed. When ready, they should be just tender, but still have some "bite"; this will take 8–10 minutes, depending on the thickness of the stems. Lift out carefully and lay flat on a warmed plate before removing the string.

Asparagus Tart
A classic quiche made with freshly gathered home-grown asparagus—and, if possible, with your own eggs—is a gastronomic experience, a far cry from mass-produced freezer food, or even a home-made tart made with commercially grown asparagus. You will really taste the difference!

SERVES 4

1 recipe quantity Shortcrust Dough (see page 150)

1 tablespoon butter or margarine

2 tablespoons grated onion or shallot

1 tablespoon chopped fresh tarragon or parsley

2 eggs

½ cup light cream

salt and freshly ground black pepper

½ cup diced Gruyère cheese (optional)

8–10 fresh asparagus spears, steamed (see page 84)

Roll out the dough thinly, and use to line a 9-inch flan pan.

Melt the butter or margarine, and cook the grated onion or shallot in it until soft, about 3–4 minutes. Remove from the heat, and stir in the tarragon or parsley. Beat in the eggs with the cream, and season well. If you want a richer dish, add the diced Gruyère cheese at this point.

Arrange the cooked asparagus spears on the bottom of the pastry shell, pour the egg and cream mixture over the top, and bake in a preheated oven at 350°F for 40 minutes. Cool a little on a wire rack, and serve warm.

Asparagus Frittata
Some gardeners like to grow asparagus as much for its decorative fern in late summer and fall, as for its succulent stems. Whether you choose to grow it in the herbaceous border or in the vegetable garden, this frittata—a Mediterranean omelet— is an easy way of enjoying your crop.

SERVES 2–3

1 lb asparagus, washed and woody part of stems
  removed

2 tablespoons high quality olive oil

4 eggs

4 tablespoons grated Pecorino or Parmesan cheese

salt and freshly ground black pepper

Steam the asparagus until just tender (see page 84). Cut into 1-inch lengths. Heat half the olive oil in a heavy-bottomed pan, and toss the asparagus in it over moderate heat for 2 minutes. Remove from the pan and drain.

Beat the eggs, and fold in the cheese. Season to taste. Add the asparagus, and mix well. Add the remaining oil to the pan, heat gently, then pour in the egg mixture. Cook over moderate heat until the bottom is nicely browned. Then slide the frittata onto a plate, and toss back into the pan so that the uncooked side is on the bottom of the pan. Cook until the underside is golden, and serve immediately.

Lettuces

Lettuces are mentioned in a fifteenth century book on gardening, at which time they were more likely to be eaten cooked along with other "pot herbs," rather than in salads. They make a very appetizing cooked vegetable, lightly braised—in crêpes, for example, or in soup—in both cases combined with peas: The combination is legendary. You can also add shredded lettuce to stir-fry dishes.

A fair herb, that men call lettuce.

S. England Legends, Anon, 1290

The Elizabethans began to eat lettuce raw, and salad came into high fashion in the sixteenth century. Was this perhaps because—they claimed—lettuce was an aphrodisiac? The Romans, on the other hand, maintained that lettuce upheld morals, and engendered temperance and chastity. The Greeks, however, valued it for its soporific qualities, and right through to the twentieth century this has been its folklore. In *Food In England* (1954) Dorothy Hartley writes:

... the expressed juice of the lettuce is one of the oldest soporifics. The juice was dried on plates, and afterward bound into white cakes. It was given to patients before and after surgical operations in conjunction with poppy seeds.

John Evelyn, writing in the seventeenth century, wrote that the lettuce "ever was and still continues the principal foundation of the universal Tribe of Salads: Which is to cool and refresh." In his *Acetaria* (1699), he developed his theory of good salad-making:

In the composure of a salad every plant should come in to bear its part, without being overpowered by some herb of a stronger taste ... but fall into their places, like the notes in music, in which there should be nothing harsh or grating.

This advice can hardly be improved upon. Nowadays there are many salad vegetables to choose from. Varieties of lettuce alone include Iceberg, Romaine, Webb's Wonder, Cabbage lettuce, Oak Leaf, Endive (Frisée), Butternut, Little Gem, and Lollo Rosso, to name but some.

Supplemented with a selection of wonderful crisp Belgian endive, celery, cucumber, scallions, as well as other leaves and fresh herbs, we are spoiled for choice. So choose your ingredients, making sure they are fresh and clean, and after washing, shake them dry in a spinner or clean towel.

Toss them in a good dressing, using the best-quality olive oil as is possible, ideally that golden-green olive oil of the first pressing: "Smooth, light and pleasant upon the tongue" (John Evelyn again). Mix the oil with the best wine or herb vinegar, some sea salt and top quality mustard, of which Dijon takes my prize. Some people like to put a pinch of sugar into dressings, too, and sometimes some crushed garlic. But don't be heavy handed on either: Keep the vinaigrette delicate, and adjust according to your taste (see basic Vinaigrette recipe on page 155).

Lambs' Lettuce and Beet Salad
Lambs' lettuce was given this name by John Gerard in his Herbal *of 1597. One country name for it is corn salad—mâche in French.*

Serves 4

¼ lb lambs' lettuce, washed

½ recipe quantity Vinaigrette (see page 155)

1 large beet, boiled and peeled

1 small apple, peeled and grated

1 hard-cooked egg, finely chopped

Toss the lambs' lettuce with the Vinaigrette. Cut the beet into thin strips, then toss into the salad with the grated apple. Scatter the finely chopped egg over the top, and serve.

Lambs' Lettuce and Baby Spinach Salad
Lambs' lettuce is a tender, tasty addition to the summer salad bowl, and this is a salad of some elegance.

Serves 4

¼ lb each lambs' lettuce and baby spinach leaves, washed

a few fresh sorrel leaves, torn

1 tablespoon chopped fresh herbs

½ recipe quantity Vinaigrette (see page 155)

½ cup finely diced Gruyère cheese

Tear any large lambs' lettuce and baby spinach leaves into smaller pieces and mix together with the herbs. Toss in the Vinaigrette. Add the diced cheese and toss again.

Salade des Vignerons
A rustic recipe from France, this unusual appetizer is a mixture of salad leaves with a hot dressing poured over it, tossed and served immediately. The flavor of the lambs' lettuce is wonderful with the touch of beet and the vinegary dressing.

¼ lb lambs' lettuce, washed

½ medium endive (frisée lettuce), washed

a few young dandelion leaves, blanched

1 medium beet, boiled and peeled, and cut

   into strips

salt and freshly ground black pepper

5 tablespoons olive oil

3 tablespoons white wine vinegar

Dry the salad leaves well, and place in a salad bowl. Put the beet in the center, and season with salt and pepper.

Heat the olive oil until just smoking, and pour over the salad. Quickly add the white wine vinegar to the hot pan, sizzle it, and when it foams pour quickly over the salad. Toss and serve the salad immediately.

Other SALAD LEAVES

Landcress and rocket grow very easily in a vegetable patch. Both have a long summer season, and are excellent salad leaves. Rocket has a particularly distinctive peppery taste.

Watercress
There is a well-known old wives' tale claiming that watercress purifies the blood, and so in the old days it was recommended as a spring salad after a long gray winter. It is indeed a valuable salad leaf, rich in iron, crisp, and with a peppery bite to its flavor. Its deep green turns to delicate bronze as the leaf matures, and always looks beautiful with a mixture of other greens in a salad bowl.

Watercress is the perfect accompaniment to a cheese board—its peppery tang is the perfect foil for mild cheeses, such as Monterey Jack and Gouda. Don't chill watercress, however—it goes limp. Just wash it, and keep in a bowl of cold water until ready to use.

Sorrel Raw, the leaves of sorrel are an excellent thirst-quencher. "The mower gladly chews it down," writes John Clare in the *Shepherd's Calendar* (1827), "and slakes his thirst as best he may."

Sorrel Soup

Sorrel, with its lemony flavor and sharp bite, can be used in the same way as spinach in soufflés and quiches, and is delicious added to a herb omelet. Use the young raw leaves in salads and sandwiches. Here it makes a lively and refreshing soup for hot weather. It is delicious served with warm crusty rolls.

SERVES 4

½ onion, peeled and finely sliced

3 tablespoons butter or margarine

2 medium potatoes, peeled and diced

4 cups Vegetable Stock (see page 156)

salt, freshly ground black pepper, and ground nutmeg

2 handfuls of fresh sorrel leaves, washed and stalks removed

3–4 tablespoons *crème fraîche*

Croûtons (see page 155), to serve

Cook the onion in the butter or margarine in a saucepan until soft. Add the diced potatoes, and stir until coated. Pour in the stock, season, and simmer gently until the potatoes are soft, 12–15 minutes.

Remove the central ribs from the sorrel leaves, and place the leaves in a blender or food processor. Pour the hot soup base over, and blend until smooth (do this with a little of the soup base at a time). Return to the clean pan, reheat, and check the seasoning. Serve with a swirl of *crème fraîche* (or sour cream) in each bowl, and scatter the top with Croûtons before handing around.

You can make a green soup of sorrel, lettuce and watercress in the same way.

Simple SORREL SAUCE

This sauce is simplicity itself to make, and freezes well. Its lemony sharpness gives a pleasing balance to grilled fish or chicken, and is excellent with poached eggs,

Remove the stalks from the sorrel leaves, and wash them. Put into a saucepan, without any added water, with a pat of margarine or butter, and cook gently until the sorrel becomes a soft mass. Chop finely, and remove any stringy bits. Thin out with a little stock and/or cream, and it is ready to serve.

$\mathscr{S}pinach$

The first record of spinach comes from China, although it was the Persians who developed its cultivation in the sixth century. It travelled via North Africa to Spain, where it was being grown by the eleventh century. Its great taste and nutritional richness (lots of iron and vitamins) have helped it to remain a firm favorite with the gardener and cook alike.

What a world of gammon and spinnage it is, though, ain't it!

David Copperfield, Charles Dickens, 1850

Spinach Roulade

The sight of a roulade can be so impressive as to be daunting. But with careful handling and precise timing, it turns out easily and is a wonderful meal served with salad, such as the Cottage Garden Salad on page 57.

SERVES 4

6 scallions, trimmed and finely chopped

1 cup cottage cheese, drained

½ recipe quantity Béchamel Sauce (see page 154)

salt, freshly ground black pepper, and ground
  nutmeg

½ lb cooked fresh spinach, finely chopped

4 eggs, separated

1 tablespoon grated Gruyère cheese

1 tablespoon grated Parmesan cheese

1 recipe quantity Fresh Tomato Sauce (see
  page 102), to serve

Fold the chopped scallions into the cottage cheese with 4 tablespoons of the Béchamel Sauce. Cook gently for 3 minutes, and season to taste with salt, pepper, and nutmeg. Set on one side.

Blend the spinach in a blender or food processor with the rest of the Béchamel Sauce and the egg yolks. Season to taste, and stir in the grated cheeses. Whisk the egg whites until stiff, and gently fold in. Line a 13 x 9 inch jelly roll pan with aluminum foil and grease it well. Spread the spinach mixture over it evenly, and bake in a preheated oven at 375°F for 15 minutes.

Remove from the oven, put a clean cloth over the top, and invert onto a flat surface. Leave for 5 minutes, then lift off the pan and remove the aluminum foil.

Spread with the cottage cheese mixture, leaving a margin around the edges. Ease carefully into a roll, using the cloth to lift it. Then flip the roulade onto a warm serving dish so that it sits with the seam underneath. Serve with Fresh Tomato Sauce.

Oeufs Florentines *The classic way of using spinach as a bed for lightly poached eggs.*

SERVES 2

¾ lb fresh spinach, cooked and drained

4 poached eggs

½ recipe quantity Béchamel Sauce (see page 154)

½ cup grated Cheddar cheese

2 tablespoons grated Parmesan cheese

Make a bed of the still-warm spinach in the bottom of a gratin dish, or in two individual cocotte dishes. Arrange the lightly poached eggs on top.

Heat the Béchamel Sauce gently, and stir in the Cheddar cheese until melted. Coat the eggs and spinach with the sauce, and sprinkle with the grated Parmesan cheese. Put under a hot broiler for a minute or so, until the top browns and the dish bubbles. Serve immediately.

Cabbage The cabbage has a long history, having been eaten in Britain by the ancient Celts and Romans. In his *Satires,* Juvenal wrote "that cabbage hashed up again and again proves the death of the wretched teachers," and the poor cabbage has never lived down its links with institutional food, invariably boiled to extinction. There are, however, some refined ways of cooking cabbage.

Red Cabbage with Apple *Braised red cabbage, cooked very slowly in the oven with stock and apples, and perhaps a little red wine, makes robust food for a hearty supper on a cold winter's night. It goes extremely well with game birds and mashed potatoes.*

SERVES 6

1 small head red cabbage, washed and sliced

2–3 Macintosh apples, cored and sliced

salt and freshly ground black pepper

2 cups Vegetable Stock (see page 154)

2–3 tablespoons red wine (optional)

Layer the red cabbage with the apples in an ovenproof casserole dish, seasoning as you go. Cover with stock, and add a little red wine if you like. Cover the casserole dish with aluminum foil and also a lid, and cook 2 hours in a preheated oven at 325°F for 1½–2 hours, turning with a wooden spoon halfway through the time. You can also layer ½ lb of chestnuts (dried ones do well) with the cabbage and apple, for a fuller, richer dish.

Cabbage SALADS

Fourteenth century physicians recommended those with weak heads for drink to chew cabbage leaves. So presumably all these salads would have a similar preventive effect! In any case, crisp white cabbage makes an excellent salad ingredient for winter, and there are endless variations that you can experiment with, using nuts and seeds and fruit, as well as other vegetables, either raw or lightly cooked. Here are a few suggestions:

• Shredded cabbage with grated horseradish, chopped onion, and radishes, in Vinaigrette (see page 155)

• Finely shredded cabbage with grated cheese, grated carrot, raisins, and chopped apple, in a coleslaw dressing (equal quantities of Mayonnaise [see page 122], yogurt, and lemon juice, seasoned with salt and pepper)

• Shredded cabbage with chopped celery, sliced red bell peppers, and raw onion rings, in Vinaigrette (see page 155)

• Shredded cabbage with chopped dried apricots that have been soaked in orange juice, chopped walnuts, and orange segments, in Mayonnaise (see page 122) or Vinaigrette (see page 155)

• Shredded cabbage with very finely sliced raw Brussels sprouts and turnips

Bubble and Squeak

The first Savoy cabbages arrived in England from Holland in the 1570s: "Tis scarce 100 years since we had Cabbages out of Holland, Sir Arthur Ashley, of Wilburg St Giles, in Dorsetshire, being the first who planted them in England," says the Gardener's Book *of 1699. I have a hunch that Bubble and Squeak is probably about as old, so firmly entrenched is it in the traditions of English cookery,*

YOU WILL NEED: • cooked potatoes • cooked cabbage, chopped • onion, chopped • meat dripping or margarine • salt and freshly ground black pepper

Put the potatoes through a ricer, or mash them well. Mix thoroughly with the chopped cabbage. Cook the onion in margarine or meat dripping and, when soft and lightly browned, press in the cabbage and potato mixture evenly. Sprinkle with salt and pepper. Cook gently. When well crusted and deep brown on the underside—this will take about 10–15 minutes—turn and brown the other side. Invert onto a heated dish.

This makes a perfect supper dish by the fireside in winter, served with fried eggs and some warm, crusty home-made bread.

Brussels Sprouts

It is thought that Brussels sprouts originated in the thriving market gardens of the Low Countries during the Middle Ages. They are miniature cabbages in bud form, growing up the stem of a plant derived from the wild cabbage, and have a strong distinctive flavor. Sprouts have long been popular in winter cookery —their season lasts from September to April—and they are traditionally an integral part of an English Christmas dinner. They quick-freeze very well, retaining their color, taste, and texture.

Pan-Fried Brussels Sprouts

Escoffier's version of this goes: "Throw them into an omelet pan containing some very hot butter and toss them in until they are nicely frizzled." It is a brilliant idea: This otherwise fairly mundane vegetable is vastly improved by this way of cooking.

Brussels sprouts, trimmed and washed	butter or margarine
salt and freshly ground black pepper	

Cook the sprouts in boiling salted water, then drain well. Melt a large pat of butter or margarine in a pan until it is very hot, put in the sprouts, and toss over brisk heat for 3–4 minutes, shaking the pan. Season with lots of black pepper.

As a variation, you can chop the sprouts up first, stew them until well softened, and then combine with as much cream as you like.

Purée of BRUSSELS SPROUTS

This is nothing less than epicurean, a revelation. It seems inconceivable that this dish is produced from the ordinary little Brussels sprout.

Cook sprouts in as little water as possible, for as short a time as possible, so they are cooked through but still slightly crunchy. Put into a blender or food processor with a little cooking liquid and some cream. Whizz to a wonderful green purée, season to taste with salt, freshly ground black pepper, and ground nutmeg, and thin out with more cream or cooking liquid as necessary.

This is delicious served with an omelet or Kookoo (see page 123).

Globe Artichokes The globe artichoke—"noble

thistle" according to John Evelyn—looks sculptural and dignified in the vegetable patch. It has

a fine, delicate flavor, and was once regarded as an aphrodisiac, which is probably the reason

why it featured quite frequently in Renaissance feasts!

Stuffed Artichokes *For a party piece, serve globe artichokes like this, with a delectable*

stuffing of lightly spiced, minced mushrooms, set on a bed of lightly dressed salad leaves.

SERVES 2

2 large globe artichokes

½ lb button mushrooms, wiped

3 scallions, trimmed and finely sliced

1 teaspoon mild curry paste or powder

squeeze of lemon juice

3–4 tablespoons Mayonnaise (see page 122)

mixed salad leaves

Vinaigrette (see page 155)

Trim the stems off the artichokes, cutting them flush with the bottom. Remove the tough outer leaves, and trim the sharp pointed tips off the remaining leaves. Cook the artichokes in boiling water, covered, for 30–40 minutes, until tender. Drain and cool. When cool enough to handle, carefully pull back the leaves of each artichoke to expose the fibrous inner center—the "choke." Carefully scrape away the choke, and discard.

Put the mushrooms in a blender or food processor, and process until they are finely minced. Steam with the sliced scallions in the microwave, or in a steamer. Cool, then drain well. Mix in the curry paste, lemon juice, and Mayonnaise, and pile into the center of the dechoked artichokes.

To serve, arrange each stuffed artichoke decoratively on a bed of mixed salad leaves, which have been lightly dressed in Vinaigrette. Dip each leaf into the mushroom filling as you eat, and finish off any remaining filling with the tender artichoke heart.

Left: *Stuffed artichokes*

B r o c c o l i
Broccoli is, to my taste, as indeed to many others, the king of the *Brassica* family. Its wonderful flavor is good hot or cold, and it goes well with numerous other ingredients, making it a versatile and welcome addition to the vegetable patch.

Broccoli and Pasta Gratin
This pasta gratin is a huge favorite with my family and has been for many years.

SERVES 4

3 cups pasta shapes, such as twists, shells, bows, or
  quills

1 lb broccoli spears

salt, freshly ground black pepper, and ground
  nutmeg

1½ recipe quantities Béchamel Sauce (see page 154)

2 teaspoons chopped tarragon or 1 teaspoon dried

4 tablespoons white wine

6 tablespoons *crème fraîche* or sour cream

2 tablespoons grated Parmesan cheese

½ cup fine dry bread crumbs

butter or margarine

Cook the pasta and broccoli separately in boiling salted water until they are tender but still have "bite." Put the cooked pasta in the bottom of a buttered gratin dish. Cover with broccoli. Heat the Béchamel Sauce gently, and add the tarragon, white wine, *crème fraîche* (or sour cream), and seasoning to taste. Stir in the cheese. Pour this sauce over the pasta and broccoli and sprinkle with the bread crumbs. Dot with butter or margarine, and bake in a preheated oven at 375°F for 25 minutes, until it bubbles at the edges and is golden brown on top.

Broccoli Soup
A simple soup, rather more like a thick purée, of broccoli and stock makes a wonderful light lunch at almost any time of the year, eaten with wholewheat pita bread. The soup freezes very well, so make lots of it if you ever have a glut of broccoli.

SERVES 2–3

2 lb broccoli, cooked until tender

3 cups Vegetable Stock (see page 154)

salt, freshly ground black pepper, and ground
  nutmeg

yogurt, to serve (optional)

Put the cooked broccoli into a blender or food processor with the stock, and blend to a smooth purée. Heat through, and season to taste with salt, pepper, and nutmeg. Serve the soup hot with a swirl of yogurt in the center if you like.

Cauliflower

"Coleflower" means "cabbage flower." It was first cultivated in medieval times—records show that cauliflowers were being grown in Europe in the thirteenth century. Closely related to calabrese and broccoli—officially slow-maturing winter cauliflowers—summer and fall cauliflowers are now widely grown. They are immensely popular for their delicate flavor, and are a versatile vegetable. You can eat cauliflower raw in salads, or cooked with any variety of sauces, or frittered, and it is famously good in pickles.

Cauliflower Soup

"Cauliflower juice in vinegar" was, so they claimed in medieval times, a cure for a hangover. It sounds so awful that I would advise avoiding the hangover, and drinking this soup instead. It makes a wonderful lunchtime warmer throughout winter.

SERVES 2–3

1 medium cauliflower

3 cups Vegetable Stock (see page 154)

1 tablespoon mild curry powder

sea salt

Steam the cauliflower until tender—a microwave gives very good results. Purée, stems and all, with a little cooking liquid and the stock, in a blender or food processor. When smooth, add the curry powder, and blend again until well amalgamated, thinning out to the desired consistency with more stock if necessary. Heat through, and season with a little sea salt. Serve hot.

You can garnish each bowl of soup with some tiny pieces of raw cauliflower, or sprinkle with roasted flaked almonds, if you wish.

Cauliflower SALADS

Raw cauliflower florets are an excellent basis for many delicious salads. Here are a few suggestions:

• With chopped hazelnuts, in Vinaigrette (see page 155) made with hazelnut or walnut oil

• Raw florets alone, in a dressing of yogurt mixed with *Moutarde de Meaux*, or garlic mayonnaise

• With crisp snow peas and waxy potatoes, in Mayonnaise (see page 122) flavored with a little curry powder

Cauliflower Noisette

Nut butter, or beurre noisette, *is made by simply heating butter or margarine until it is so hot that it turns nut-brown and has, indeed, a nutty taste. It has a special affinity with cauliflower, one of the finest vegetables on the patch. You can make this with or without cheese.*

SERVES 4–6

1 large cauliflower, broken into florets

salt

1 stick margarine or butter

½ cup finely grated Gruyère cheese

flaked almonds, toasted, to garnish

Cook the cauliflower in boiling salted water, so that it still has "bite." Drain well. Heat the butter or margarine in a thick pan until it turns a light hazelnut color.

Put the cauliflower into a buttered heatproof dish, and sprinkle with the finely grated Gruyère. Heat through under the broiler and, just before serving, spoon the warm *beurre noisette* over the top.

Eggplant

This glossy, smooth-skinned fruit is a member of the nightshade family and probably originated in India. Eggplants range through purple to whitish-cream in color, and grow in tropical and subtropical zones all the year round. They were adopted by the British when the Indians—who call them "brinjal"—introduced them to their rulers under the Raj. They are known as "eggplant" because of their shape.

Eggplant with Pasta and Cheese

If you are successful at growing your own eggplants, the traditional ways to cook them are in moussaka, or fried in olive oil, or as fritters. But, to beat them all, try this recipe.

SERVES 4

2 medium eggplants

salt and freshly ground black pepper

olive oil for frying

1 cup Fresh Tomato Sauce (see page 102)

2 cups pasta shapes, such as twists, shells, or quills, cooked *al dente*

2 cups finely grated Cheddar or Pecorino cheese

1–2 garlic cloves, peeled and crushed

Cut the eggplants into thin slices, and sprinkle with salt. Let sweat for 30 minutes, then wipe dry. Cook the slices gently in olive oil until soft and lightly browned on both sides: They will absorb a lot of oil so keep the pan replenished.

Butter an ovenproof dish, and cover the bottom with a thin layer of Fresh Tomato Sauce. Cover with a layer of eggplant, then a layer of pasta, then a layer of grated cheese, seasoning with garlic, salt, and pepper as you go. Continue layering until all the ingredients are used up, finishing with a layer of cheese. Bake in a preheated oven at 350°F for 25 minutes. Serve immediately.

Tomatoes The tomato is a native of Mexico, and its name comes from their *tomatl.* In spite of being related to the deadly nightshade and thought at first to be poisonous, tomatoes survived rural superstition to become one of our most popular vegetables.

Summer Tomato Soup *When your tomato crop is at its height in summer, this soup is a wonderful way of using it, and it also freezes extremely well.*

SERVES 6

1 onion, peeled and finely chopped	1 tablespoon tomato paste
1½ lb tomatoes, coarsely chopped	a few thin strips of orange rind
2 garlic cloves, peeled and finely chopped	1 small bayleaf
2 tablespoons butter or margarine	2 tablespoons chopped fresh parsley
3 cups Vegetable Stock (see page 154)	salt and freshly ground black pepper
	1 tablespoon chopped fresh tarragon, to garnish

Cook the chopped onions, tomatoes, and garlic very gently in the butter or margarine in a covered pan, stirring occasionally, for about 20 minutes, until very soft. Purée in a blender or food processor.

Return to the pan with the stock, tomato paste, strips of orange rind, bayleaf, and parsley. Bring to a boil, then season to taste. Simmer very gently for 10 minutes, then remove the bayleaf. Serve hot or chilled. Just before serving, stir in the chopped tarragon.

Tomato Tart

The first tomatoes were yellow, and were widely known as the "golden apple" (thought to be a dangerous love potion with special magic). The Italian for tomato still reflects this: Pomodoro *is a literal translation. It was the Italians who invented the ultimate tomato tart, the pizza, but here is an old English version which makes a welcome change.*

SERVES 4–6

1 recipe quantity Shortcrust Dough (see page 150)

1½ lb tomatoes, sliced

salt and freshly ground black pepper

1 cup pinhead oatmeal

olive oil for frying

a large bunch fresh basil, chopped

3 tablespoons grated Cheddar cheese

Roll out the dough, and use to line a 9-inch tart pan. Season the tomato slices with salt and pepper. Dip in the oatmeal until well coated, then sauté them in olive oil until the oatmeal forms a golden crust. Pile into the tart shell, making layers with the basil. Sprinkle the cheese over the top, and bake in a preheated oven at 425°F for 15 minutes, then at 375°F for a further 2 minutes. Cool a little on a wire rack before serving.

Fresh Tomato Sauce

Tomato sauce has long been popular in English food, both rural and urban: "Chops and Tomato Sauce. Yours, Pickwick," writes Charles Dickens in the Pickwick Papers *(1836), and what has changed? Making this sauce with your own sun-ripened tomatoes is the best of all, so make lots when your annual crop is at its height, and freeze it for use throughout the year.*

MAKES 3 CUPS

1 lb very ripe tomatoes, peeled (see below)

medium bunch fresh mixed herbs, such as parsley, tarragon, savory, thyme, chervil, sage, etc.

4 scallions trimmed and sliced

1½ cups canned tomato juice or Vegetable Stock (see page 154), or a mixture of both

salt and freshly ground black pepper

Remove any tough stem from the centers of the tomatoes, and chop the flesh coarsely. Put into a blender or food processor with the herbs and scallions. Whizz to a paste. Add the tomato juice and/or stock, and heat through very gently for 10 minutes. Season to taste with salt and pepper.

TO PEEL TOMATOES: Cover with boiling water, and leave for 2–3 minutes. Then pierce with a sharp knife, and the skin will peel off easily.

Right: *Fresh tomato sauce*

Lima Beans Lima beans are one of mankind's oldest cultivated vegetables, and are especially renowned for their affinity with bacon. In the words of G. K. Chesterton, in *The Englishman*, 1902:

But since he stood for England

And knew what England means,

Unless you give him bacon

You must not give him beans.

Lima beans are exquisite eaten young, cooked with a sprig of parsley which brings out their flavor, just as a sprig of mint enhances peas. Serve them hot, buttered, or with a little cream, or cold in salads during early summer.

Lima Bean and Mushroom Salad *The contrasting flavors and textures of lima beans and mushrooms make this a particularly memorable salad.*

SERVES 3–4

½ lb small, shelled lima beans, cooked

1½ cups button mushrooms, wiped and
   thinly sliced

1–2 teaspoons curry powder

1–2 tablespoons Vinaigrette (see page 155)

small bunch fresh cilantro, finely chopped

Mix together the cooked lima beans and sliced mushrooms in a serving bowl. Mix the curry powder to taste into the Vinaigrette. Pour over the vegetables, toss all together with the chopped cilantro, and serve slightly chilled.

Lima Bean Soup *The strong, earthy flavor of lima beans is wonderful in soup, especially made with the young, whole pods and served with a sprinkling of summer herbs. Serve with warm wholewheat bread.*

SERVES 4–6

2 lb small young lima beans, whole, cleaned

2 scallions, trimmed

a handful of outer lettuce leaves, washed and torn

4 cups Vegetable Stock (see page 154)

1 cup milk

3 tablespoons heavy cream

chopped fresh summer savory or mint, to garnish

Put the lima beans, scallions, and torn lettuce leaves into a big pan. Cover with stock, and simmer until tender, about 12–15 minutes. Strain, reserving the liquid. Put the beans into a blender or food processor with enough of the liquid to blend to a smooth, thick soup. Add the milk, reheat, and then stir in the cream. Sprinkle with chopped summer savory or mint just before serving.

Snow peas
You eat snow peas whole. They are good, both lightly cooked and raw, in salads, especially mixed with ripe avocado. Sometimes they are referred to as "mangetout" or "sugar peas."

Stir-Fried Snow Peas
Snow peas are delicious stir-fried, retaining all their crispness, flavor and color. You can put them into a mixed stir-fry of summer vegetables, or simply cook them on their own as here, with ginger, garlic, and black bean sauce.

SERVES 3–4

3 tablespoons peanut oil

1 lb snow peas, cleaned

2 tablespoons soy sauce

½ inch root ginger, peeled and finely grated

1 medium garlic clove, peeled and crushed

1–2 teaspoons black bean sauce, to taste

3 tablespoons dark sesame oil

Heat the peanut oil in a wok or large skillet, and toss in the snow peas. Stir-fry over high heat until heated through but still crisp. Turn the heat down, add the soy sauce, and cover the pan. Cook gently for a few minutes, until the snow peas soften a little. Meanwhile, combine the grated ginger, crushed garlic, black bean sauce, and dark sesame oil. Stir this mixture into the snow peas, cook for a further minute or so to heat through, and then serve.

Runner Beans
The only way to eat these delectable beans is young, fresh from the vine, shredded, or finely sliced (diagonally), then boiled or steamed until just tender and served with a pat of butter. Wonderful! On the whole they don't respond to the alchemy of *haute cuisine*, so keep them simple.

Corn
Corn was first grown as a crop in Mexico as far back as 7000 BC, and the South Americans still grow many varieties, including a purple Peruvian corn. It was the principal food of the Aztec, Mayan, and Inca Indians of South America, and it was they who first discovered popcorn!

Corn Fines Herbes
Ears of corn are always best straight from the stalk, freshly picked, and simply plunged into boiling water. Traditionally served just with melted butter, this addition of fresh herbs is a delectable improvement.

SERVES 4

4 ears corn

1 stick butter or margarine

4 tablespoons finely chopped mixed fresh herbs, such as basil, dill, thyme, cilantro, marjoram, mint, chives, etc., or 2 tablespoons dried herbs

sea salt

Shuck the corn. Spread with softened butter or margarine, and roll in very finely chopped fresh herbs of your choice. Sprinkle with a little sea salt. Wrap in aluminum foil, and bake in a preheated oven at 350°F for 15 minutes. Serve in the foil packet, rolling in the buttery herby juices before you take each bite.

Corn à la Crème
A simple dish of corn mixed with herbs and crème fraîche *makes a delicious side vegetable. To make a more substantial dish, you can lay the creamed corn on a bed of rice, and bake it in the same way. It is wonderful, and a complete meal in itself with tossed mixed salad.*

SERVES 4

4 corn ears, or 1 lb canned corn, drained

½ cup *crème fraîche* or sour cream

½ cup light cream

salt and freshly ground black pepper

2 tablespoons butter or margarine

4 tablespoons finely chopped mixed fresh herbs, such as basil, dill, thyme, cilantro or marjoram

Scrape the corn off the ears if using fresh, or use canned corn, and mix into the *crème fraîche* or sour cream and single cream. Add the chopped herbs and season to taste. Rub a gratin dish with the butter or margarine, and add the corn mixture. Bake in a preheated oven at 325°F for 35–45 minutes, until golden. Serve hot.

Baby Corn with Cilantro
This dish of baby ears is out of this world, truly epicurean, and I have had many a demand for the recipe. It goes beautifully as a side dish to accompany the Asparagus Tart on page 85.

SERVES 4

5 tablespoons olive oil

1 lb baby ears of corn

4–5 scallions, trimmed and finely chopped

small bunch fresh cilantro, finely chopped

2 garlic cloves, peeled and crushed

1 inch root ginger, peeled and grated

1 cup *crème fraîche* or sour cream

sprigs of fresh cilantro, to garnish

Heat half the oil in a large pan, and gently turn the baby ears of corn in it for 6–7 minutes, stirring all the time. Cover with a lid and let steam for 5 minutes. Remove the corn from the pan when it begins to soften. Add more oil to the pan, stir in the scallions, and sauté gently until soft, about 5 minutes. Add the chopped cilantro, garlic, and ginger, and stir-fry for a further 2 minutes. Return the baby ears of corn to the pan, and cook gently, covered, stirring from time to time, for a further 10 minutes. Remove from the heat, and allow to cool for 5 minutes. Then stir in the *crème fraîche* or sour cream. Serve warm or cold, garnished with sprigs of cilantro.

Green Beans
The French bean, a tender annual variety of the green bean genus, probably originated in South America but has long been cultivated in many other tropical, subtropical, and temperate areas of the world. Green beans were brought back to Europe by the conquering Spanish, and cultivated specially by the French, hence the name of one of the finest species. There are many varieties of green bean, two of which mature to provide the kidney and haricot beans. French beans are closely related to the Scarlet Runner Bean.

Green Beans à la Française
This is how Eliza Acton cooked green beans in the nineteenth century, and very good it is too: A simple, lemony fresh side dish with a classic feel to it. It is delicious with grilled fish and tossed salad.

SERVES 4

1½ lb green beans, cleaned

2 tablespoons butter or margarine

1 tablespoon flour

salt and freshly ground black pepper

½ cup Vegetable Stock (see page 154)

2 egg yolks

1 tablespoon lemon juice

Simmer the beans until tender, about 8 minutes, and then drain them. In a fresh pan, melt the butter or margarine, and stir in the flour until smooth. When lightly browned, season with salt and pepper, and gradually pour in the stock, stirring until smooth. Add the beans and toss. Off the heat, stir in the egg yolks and lemon juice, and serve at once.

Green Bean and Cauliflower Salad
As a summer salad this is hard to improve upon. The touch of mint and garlic in the dressing of quality olive oil and lemon juice gives extra zest to the fresh, crisp vegetables. Serve it as an appetizer, with fresh wholewheat bread, or as part of a buffet table.

SERVES 4–6

1 small cauliflower, divided into florets

½ lb green beans, cleaned

2 tablespoons finely chopped fresh mint

1–2 garlic cloves, peeled and crushed

5 tablespoons olive oil

1–2 tablespoons lemon juice

sea salt

Simmer the cauliflower and beans separately, until tender but still slightly crisp. Drain well, and arrange in a shallow dish. Sprinkle with the chopped mint. Add the crushed garlic to the olive oil, and mix in lemon juice and sea salt to taste. Pour this dressing evenly over the vegetables, and leave in a cool place for 30 minutes to 1 hour before serving. Do not chill.

Peas Tiny young peas,

fresh from the garden and cooked with

mint, are deservedly popular side veg-

etables. Try the following recipes, too.

Q: How do you boil peas?

A: Briskly, ma'am.

Finchley Manual for the Training of Servants, 1800

Risi e Bisi *A simple dish of Italian inspiration, this makes a satisfying meal served with tossed salad.*

SERVES 4–6

3 tablespoons butter or margarine

1 small onion, finely chopped

2¼ cups shelled garden peas

3 cups Vegetable Stock (see page 154)

¾ cup basmati rice

1 teaspoon dried oregano

grated Parmesan cheese, to serve

Melt the butter or margarine, and cook the onion very gently, covered, for about 10 minutes, stirring from time to time, until soft. Stir in the peas, and when covered with the fat, pour in half the stock. When it is bubbling, add the rice, the rest of the stock, and the oregano. Cook gently, covered with a lid, for about 10 minutes. Check that it does not dry out, adding more stock if necessary. Stir as little as possible, otherwise the peas will break up. When the rice is cooked, serve, passing a bowl of grated Parmesan cheese separately.

Green Pea Soup "St Germain" *The bright, deep green color of this soup is one of the delights of midsummer. Serve it hot with garlic bread, or chilled with warm pita bread.*

SERVES 4

2¼ cups shelled garden peas

1 medium potato, peeled and sliced

1 medium onion, peeled and sliced

1 medium lettuce, quartered and washed

4 cups Vegetable Stock (see page 154)

juice of ½ lemon

½ cup light cream

salt and freshly ground black pepper

Put the peas, potato, onion, lettuce, and half the stock into a pan, and bring to a boil. Cover, and simmer for 5 minutes. Process to a fine purée in a blender or food processor. Return to the pan with the rest of the stock, and reheat. Add the lemon juice, stir well, then stir in the cream. Season to taste and serve hot or chilled.

Right: *Risi e bisi*

Zucchini

Zucchini came into English cookery in a serious way thanks to Elizabeth David: It was she who first brought it to her public in *French Provincial Cooking* in the 1960s. Zucchini is an exquisite vegetable, and if you grow just three or four plants on your vegetable patch, you will be well provided for throughout the summer. You can use them raw in salads, very finely sliced, or lightly steamed as a filling for omelets or tossed into pasta with fresh herbs and a little cream.

Zucchini Soup

A delicate green starter for summer, this version of zucchini soup is lightly flavored with fresh dill, and is excellent served either hot or chilled. I like it with Melba Toast (see page 155).

SERVES 4

4 scallions, trimmed and sliced

3 tablespoons margarine

1 lb zucchini, trimmed and thinly sliced

1 tablespoon flour

4 cups Vegetable Stock (see page 154)

salt and freshly ground black pepper

2 tablespoons chopped fresh dill

yogurt or *crème fraîche*, to serve (optional)

Gently sauté the scallions in the margarine for 4–5 minutes, until soft. Add the zucchini, and stir until coated. Cover, and leave for 5 minutes on gentle heat. Sprinkle in the flour, and then gradually add half the stock. Stir until the mixture thickens, and then simmer until the zucchini are just cooked, about 10 minutes. Purée in a blender or food processor. Return to the pan, and add the remaining stock to bring to a thin consistency. Heat through or chill, as you wish, then season to taste, and stir in the dill. Serve with a swirl of yogurt or *crème fraîche* floating on top, if you wish.

Golden POCKETS

For a late summer dish, use the flowers of ripe zucchini to make this elegant *hors d'oeuvre*.

Stuff each zucchini flower with a little stuffing (made from cooked rice or fresh bread crumbs, chopped herbs and/or a little grated cheese, seasoning, and beaten egg to bind), dip in Fritter Batter (see page 154), and deep-fry to a delicate brown. Serve garnished with baby tomatoes and sprigs of fried parsley.

Zucchini Fines Herbes *This simple, elegant way of cooking zucchini is based on a classic French recipe.*

SERVES 4

1½ lb zucchini, trimmed and
   diagonally sliced

salt

6 tablespoons butter or margarine, melted

¾ cup *crème fraîche* or sour cream

sprigs of fresh rosemary, savory, lovage, marjoram,
   fennel, etc., all finely chopped

Blanch the zucchini in boiling salted water for 3–4 minutes. Drain well, and put into a deep pan with the melted butter or margarine. Stir, cover, and let cook gently until tender, shaking the pan from time to time. Then, off the heat, stir in the *crème fraîche* or sour cream and finally the herbs. Heat through, and serve.

Zucchini Parmigiana *A great Italian dish, this is made up of layers of zucchini, tomato sauce, and cheese, baked until the top is crusty and golden brown. It makes a complete meal in itself, just served with warm wholewheat bread and tossed salad, full of herbs. This dish freezes well.*

SERVES 6

3 lb zucchini

1 recipe quantity Fresh Tomato Sauce (see
   page 102)

½ lb mozzarella cheese, sliced

salt and freshly ground black pepper

⅛ cup grated Parmesan cheese

olive oil

Trim and slice the zucchini ¼ inch thick, diagonally. Blanch in boiling water for 2–3 minutes. Drain, and arrange in layers in a deep dish with Fresh Tomato Sauce and slices of mozzarella, seasoning each layer with plenty of salt and pepper. Repeat until all the ingredients are used up. Top with the grated Parmesan, drizzle with olive oil, and bake in a preheated oven at 375°F for 40–45 minutes, until the cheese is browned and crusty. Serve immediately.

Pumpkin Cultivated since ancient times, pumpkins come in varying shapes and colors, and are a wonderful sight at Halloween.

Soup Fermière *Pumpkin soup is one of the greatest treats of early fall, warming the first chill evenings with its golden color and its full, rich flavor. A couple of sugar pumpkins in the vegetable garden will keep you supplied with this soup, which also freezes well, so you can eat it throughout the winter months.*

SERVES 6

2 lb sugar pumpkin, peeled, sliced, and seeded

salt, freshly ground black pepper, and ground nutmeg

about ½ cup milk or light cream

Croûtons (see page 155) and finely grated cheese, to serve

Cut the pumpkin flesh into chunks, and put into a pan with water to just cover. Add some salt and simmer, covered, for about 25–30 minutes, until the pumpkin is tender. Blend to a smooth purée with the cooking water in a blender or food processor, and thin out to the desired consistency with milk or cream. Heat through, and season to taste with pepper and nutmeg.

Serve with Croûtons and a bowl of finely grated cheese to sprinkle over the top.

Whole Baked Pumpkin *I know no better way than this of eating pumpkin: It is rich and delicious, soft and appetizing, and serves as a meal in itself with baked potatoes and tossed salad.*

SERVES 6

10 inch diameter sugar pumpkin

½ stick butter or margarine

sea salt and freshly ground black pepper

1½ cups light cream

Cut a lid off the pumpkin at the stalk end. Scoop out the seeds and fibers. Smear the inner surface with butter or margarine. Sprinkle sea salt and freshly ground pepper into the cavity. Replace the lid, and put into an ovenproof dish. Bake for 1 hour in a preheated oven at 375°F, until the flesh inside is soft. Remove the lid, and pour in the cream, heated until just under boiling point. Serve the pumpkin *à la crème*, scooped straight out of the shell.

Roast Pumpkin *Pumpkin can be used in sweet dishes: Spicy pumpkin pie is traditionally served at American Thanksgiving festivities. In this recipe the pumpkin is cut into small pieces and cooked like roast potatoes or parsnips: It makes a delightful change as a side vegetable for a fall Sunday lunch.*

sugar pumpkin, peeled, sliced, and seeded	salt and freshly ground black pepper
flour, sifted	oil for cooking

Cut the slices of pumpkin into small potato-size pieces, roll lightly in sifted flour, and season with salt and pepper. Arrange in a roasting pan of hot oil, or around a beef or pork roast, and baste them during the cooking time. They will take 40 minutes in a preheated oven at 375°F.

English Marrow and Squashes

This now very popular vegetable came to England at the end of the nineteenth century, so there are no old, traditional recipes for it to be found in antique cookery books. English marrows and squashes come in all shapes, sizes, and colors, from the baby vegetable marrows or zucchini so well known in European cuisine, to the wide variety of summer and winter squashes that feature extensively in American cookery. You can simply bake them, or boil them, or cook them in butter with herbs, but one of the best ways to prepare them is to stuff and then bake them, wrapped in tin foil, which makes a wonderful fall dish. A stuffing of tomatoes, brown bread crumbs, and parsley, bound with egg and well seasoned, is scrumptious. More substantially, you can fill the seed cavity with spicy beans and butter, or with spinach and cottage cheese, or you can make a rice stuffing with chopped onion, garlic, mint or dill, and a little cinnamon. One of my favorites is the buckwheat stuffing described opposite.

Autumn Stuffed English Marrow *This makes a wonderful meal for those first really cold evenings of early winter, served with buttered potatoes and some broiled tomatoes. If you cannot find marrows, this recipe works well with butternut squash.*

SERVES 4

1 teaspoon oil

¾ cup kasha

salt and freshly ground black pepper

1 tablespoon chopped mixed fresh herbs

3 scallions, trimmed and finely chopped

1 tablespoon margarine

2 medium carrots, peeled and grated

1 medium zucchini, trimmed and grated

1 large English marrow or butternut squash

Heat the oil in a skillet, and quickly sauté the kasha over high heat for 2–3 minutes, stirring all the time. Add 2 cups boiling water, cover, and simmer for 15 minutes until the kasha is soft. Season to taste, and blend in the herbs.

Sauté the scallions in the margarine until soft, add the grated carrots and zucchini, and simmer until soft. Season, and add to the kasha. Cut the marrow or butternut squash in half lengthwise, and hollow it out, removing the seeds. Fill the hollow with the kasha mixture, and press the two halves back together.

Wrap in aluminum foil and bake in a preheated oven at 350°F for 45–55 minutes, until very tender. Serve hot, cut into thick slices.

English Marrow and Pineapple Jam *This translucent, golden jam is one of the fall's delights, and remains a pleasure through the gloomy days of winter. It is delectable on toast for breakfast. This jam is equally good made with sugar pumpkins.*

MAKES 10 LB

6 lb English marrow or sugar pumpkin, peeled, halved, and seeded

1 lb canned pineapple

12 cups sugar

Cut the marrow or pumpkinflesh into small cubes, and dice the pineapple. Put in layers with the sugar in a preserving pan, and leave overnight to extract all the juices. Boil to setting point (see page 145), pour into sterilized jars and seal (see page 145). Store in a cool, dark, dry place.

You can also make this jam with ginger, adding 1-inch cube root ginger, bruised, to the cooking. Remove at the end of the cooking time, and then add some slices of crystallized ginger before canning.

eggs *Galore*

About Candlemas Day

Every good goose should lay

Traditional

Medieval English cottagers frequently kept geese, ducks, or a few chickens; they were essential suppliers of eggs and—principally—of poultry meat. Although the chickens were not big layers, as they had to scratch around for their own food, ducks and geese would provide an extra supply of rich eggs for cakes and savory meals. Eggs were used lavishly in wealthy households of old, as their recipe books show us, full of sauces and desserts using quantities of eggs and cream which seem very unhealthy now. But then, in a world without modern technology, people led more physically active lives and could tolerate a richer diet.

There is nothing fresher or better to taste than eggs from your own chickens. However, keeping them entails a job for every day of the year, so is not a hobby to be undertaken lightly. Chickens have to be fed and watered daily, and kept clean and disease free, and the eggs must be gathered regularly. But if you decide to try it, you will be rewarded with a constant supply of fresh eggs, plus usually an excess for friends and neighbors.

The HENPEN OF 1615

Your henne house would be large and spacious with somewhat a high roofe and walls strong and windowes upon the sunne rising: round about the inside of the walls upon the ground would be built large pens of 3 ft high for Geese, Ducks and fowle to sit in.

Near to the eavings ... would be perches ... on which should sit your Cocks, Hennes, Capon and Turkies, each on several perches as they are disposed...

You shall gather your eggs up once a day and leave in the nest but the nest egge, and no more, and that would ever be in the afternoon when you have seene every Henne come from the nest severally. Some Hennes will by the cackling tell you when they have layd, but some will lay mute, therefore you must let your owne eye be your instruction.

Perfect Husbandry, **Gervase Markham**, *c.*1630

THE CHICKEN COOP

More modern instructions would decree a two-story chicken coop, large enough to allow each bird 3 sq ft, set in a run of at least half an acre, since the run soon turns to mud and can become a disease risk. Site the chicken coop near a hedge or windbreak, and keep everything surrounded by chicken wire for protection. The chicken coop should contain nesting boxes, a litter area, and a perch on the second floor above a removable droppings board. The ground floor must be covered with soft wood shavings, straw, or peat moss, about 6–8 inches deep. The droppings, scraped off the boards and then dried, are rich compost material for grass, and mixed with fire ash make an excellent activator for a compost heap.

A food trough for wet mash needs to be large enough to allow 5–6 inch access for each bird. You can fit a galvanised tube feeder for dry mash feed, one tube to every 25 birds. Modern birds need special feeds packed with protein, energy, vitamins, and minerals. You can supplement this with a few household scraps, but in general these are not that nutritious and birds have small appetites. Every laying hen will eat ¼ lb dry mash per day, plus a little "scratch feed"—corn scattered around the run to keep them occupied—about 1 oz per bird per day. Some people tie outer cabbage leaves or other greens in a string bag for the birds to peck at: These not only supply vitamins and add variety, but also give a deeper color to the yolks. Water for the drinkers should be topped up every day, allowing 1 cup per bird per day.

CHICKEN MANAGEMENT

For beginners, it is advisable to buy a flock at "point-of-lay", i.e., pullets 18–20 weeks old that have been reared from day-old chicks by specialist growers. These will have been hatched in May, so you can start your flock off in early September. Once they have settled, they should lay for 12 months without a break, your first eggs appearing in October. The best birds will continue laying in their second year, but chickens are as prone to disease and predators as any other creature, so they have to be well managed. The best idea is to get a really good manual to guide you through all the pitfalls of rearing and management, broodiness and moulting, and other hazards, and you should be rewarded by a good egg harvest.

If, for example, you have six birds, you should get 4–5 eggs per day. Check the nest two or three times a day (and always knock before entering: Chickens are nervous birds and a shock can put them off laying). Eggs store well in a cool room (under 50°F) for 3–4 weeks, pointed end down. Don't store near fish, onions, or cheese, since they pick up strong smells, and don't store them in the fridge, since they deteriorate rapidly once taken out.

Before the selective breeding of chickens, management and storage were different, and the supply of eggs seasonal, as this excerpt from Markham's *Cheap and Good Husbandry* (1613) illustrates:

If you feed your Hens often with toasts taken out of ale, or with barley boiled, they will lay soon. Now because eggs of them-selves are a singular profit, you shall understand that the best way to preserve or keep them long is some think to lay them in straw, but that is too cold, and besides will make them musty; others will lay them in bran, but that will make them putre-fy; and others lay them in salt, but that makes them diminish. The best way then to keep them most sweet, sound and full, is only to keep them in a heap of malt, close and well covered all over.

Classic Egg Recipes

Fresh eggs from free-range chickens make all the difference to the flavor of your cooking. Eggs are so versatile, use them in omelets, soufflés, crêpes, and custard sauces. Leftover whites from home-made mayonnaise can be used up in meringues. And nothing is easier than scrambled or poached eggs for light meals.

Vegetable Soufflés

There is a mystique about cooking soufflés that undermines the confidence of the most committed cook, but if you follow the basic instructions given below carefully, you will succeed. There are many vegetables that make sublime soufflés, for example, spinach, sorrel, mushrooms, parsnips, zucchini and tomatoes.

SERVES 4–6

soft fresh bread crumbs

grated Parmesan cheese

1 lb vegetables, (see list above), cooked, drained, and the cooking liquid reserved

5 tablespoons Bêchamel Sauce (see page 154), made with milk or the vegetable cooking water, or both

4 egg yolks

salt and freshly ground black pepper

fresh herbs or spices to taste

5 egg whites, very stiffly beaten

Grease a 5-cup soufflé dish, then sprinkle the inside liberally with bread crumbs and grated Parmesan. Chop or purée the cooked vegetables, as required. For variety you can add a few chopped mushrooms, cooked in butter with garlic, or chopped walnuts for texture. Stir in the Bêchamel Sauce, and mix well, beat in the egg yolks, season, and add herbs or spices to taste. Fold in the stiffly beaten egg whites deftly and lightly, and pour into the prepared soufflé dish. Bake at 400°F for 25–30 minutes until well risen and golden, but still slightly runny in the center. Get everyone sitting around the table before you take it out of the oven, and eat immediately, before it sinks.

Piperade *This is my version of a traditional French dish, and it makes an excellent lunch dish, which is quickly prepared. Serve it with crusty brown bread and tossed salad.*

SERVES 3

½ stick butter or margarine

2 medium onions, peeled and finely sliced

2 garlic cloves, peeled and finely sliced

4 large ripe tomatoes, peeled (see page 102) and
  chopped

2 canned roasted red peppers, cut into strips

2 boiled potatoes, finely diced

6 eggs

salt and freshly ground black pepper

1 tablespoon chopped fresh parsley

Melt the butter or margarine in a heavy-bottomed pan, and cook the onion and garlic in it, covered, until soft, about 10 minutes. Then turn up the heat a little, and cook until they brown lightly. Add the tomatoes, the strips of pepper, and the potatoes, and cook for a further 5 minutes.

Beat the eggs lightly, and season with salt and pepper. Stir into the vegetable mixture, and continue stirring as you would for scrambled eggs, until thick and creamy but not dry. Serve immediately, sprinkled with chopped parsley.

Mayonnaise *Nothing can match home-made mayonnaise, especially if you make it with your own eggs from free-range chickens. It takes a careful hand to get it right, and patience, but it's a skill well worth acquiring .*

MAKES ABOUT 1½ CUPS

2–3 egg yolks

a pinch of salt

a pinch of dry mustard

1 cup olive oil

a few drops tarragon or wine vinegar

juice of about ½ lemon

Beat the egg yolks thoroughly in a small bowl, and then stir in the salt and mustard. Beating gently all the time, very gradually blend in the oil: At first add it drop by drop, then gradually increase the flow to a thin trickle. Go very slowly, stopping the oil from time to time (but continue beating) to allow the mayonnaise to thicken. Gradually increase the trickle, but don't go too fast, otherwise the mayonnaise will curdle. Stir in the vinegar as the mixture thickens, to thin it out slightly. Then gradually add enough lemon juice to bring to the consistency you require. Keep in a cool place, but do not refrigerate or the eggs will degrade and the mayonnaise may separate.

Omelets
Omelets and quiches are perhaps the most obvious and accessible ways of using up eggs. A quiche is a quiche, but there are nuances to and variations on the omelet that are worth exploring.

YOU WILL NEED: • **eggs (2 per person)** • **oil or butter** • **salt and freshly ground black pepper** • **cream**

For preference, use a copper-bottomed pan for making an omelet. Smear it with a little oil or butter, and set it over medium heat until very hot. Then pour in your omelet mixture: The requisite number of eggs (2 per person usually), beaten with salt and pepper, and a little cream if you wish. Pour into the pan, and when the mixture begins to bubble and blister, fold the lightly cooked edges toward the center. Do this once or twice, being careful not to let the mixture overheat and dry out, or burn on the bottom. Put the filling of your choice into the center, and flip the omelet over. Flip onto a hot plate or serving dish, and serve immediately. It should be slightly runny and creamy in the center.

KOOKOO

A solid omelet where the egg mixture is beaten into a mixture of sautéed vegetables, then cooked gently in a covered pan for 10–15 minutes until quite set. Eat it cut into wedges, with salad and new potatoes or crusty bread, or allow it to get cold and then cut into tiny squares to be served with pre-dinner drinks. It is also delicious warm. You can use potatoes, spinach, zucchini, broccoli, peas, or corn for the filling, or a mixture of some of them, sautéed with softened onions if desired.

First cook the chosen vegetables gently in olive oil or butter in the pan until soft, and then pour on the omelet mixture (see above). Cover, then let cook over gentle heat until the kookoo is set. Do not let the bottom burn. Then put under a broiler to brown the top. Invert onto a serving dish.

Sweet SOUFFLÉ OMELETS

A dessert variation made like a soufflé and cooked like an omelet, over medium to gentle heat, ensuring the bottom does not brown. Egg yolks are beaten with sugar until thick, and then the stiffly beaten whites folded in lightly. The filling—such as sugared and sliced strawberries, sweetened raspberries or slices of peach—is placed on the omelet while it is still cooking, then the omelet is flipped over the filling and cooked a little longer. If the inside is too runny to serve, put the soufflé omelet into a hot oven for 3–4 minutes, just to finish cooking. Don't put too much mixture into the pan at one time: It is best to cook these delicacies for just two people at a time. Three eggs will do four people.

Savory Crêpes

Pancake Day is one of Britain's most ancient traditions to survive more or less intact into the late twentieth century. Every Shrove Tuesday, races are run through certain villages and the participants toss pancakes (crêpes) as they go.

But hark, I hear the Pancake Bell
The fritters make a gallant smell

Poor Robin's Almanac, 1671

MAKES 12 CRÊPES

1¼ cups flour

a pinch of salt

2 large eggs

1 cup milk

½ cup water

1 teaspoon vegetable oil

oil or fat, for cooking

a little grated cheese (optional)

Filling:

a savory filling of your choice, such as creamed spinach, corn, mushrooms, and garlic: See "The Vegetable Patch" chapter for other ideas.

Sift the flour with the salt, and make a well in the center. Break the eggs into the well, and mix thoroughly with a wooden spoon. Gradually add the milk and water, mixed together, and stir until completely smooth. Stir in the oil, and let stand in a cool place for 2 hours.

To cook, lightly grease a heavy-bottomed skillet, and heat it through until pretty hot but not quite smoking. Pour 1–2 tablespoons of the batter into the pan. Immediately swirl the pan so that the batter covers the bottom evenly, and cook over medium heat until the batter is set and lightly browned. Loosen the edges and then flip the crêpe over to cook the other side. Continue until all the batter is used up, stacking the crêpes on top of each other as you take them out of the pan and keeping them warm.

Roll up some of the chosen filling inside each crêpe. Place the crêpes side by side in an ovenproof dish, sprinkle with grated cheese, if desired, and bake in a preheated oven at 350°F for 10–15 minutes, until heated through.

Sweet Crêpes
Crêpes make stylish desserts, and there are endless fillings that you can experiment with (see below). You can also vary the flavor of the crêpes themselves: Add ground ginger to the batter before cooking, or the finely grated rind of either lemon or orange. Serve the crêpes with cream or crème fraîche, *if liked.*

MAKES 10–12 CRÊPES

1 cup all-purpose flour

pinch of salt

2 tablespoons sugar

2 eggs

2 egg yolks

½ cup light cream

½ cup milk

unsalted butter for cooking

sugar for sprinkling

Filling:

a sweet filling of your choice, such as home-made
jam, soft summer fruits, stewed fruit, etc.—see
below for suggestions.

Sift the flour and salt together, and stir in the sugar. Make a well in the center of the mixture, and put the eggs and egg yolks into the well. Gradually mix in the flour, and beat until smooth. Add the cream and milk gradually until you have a smooth batter. Let stand in a cool place for at least 1 hour.

Use 1 tablespoon of the mixture to make each crêpe, cooking them in unsalted butter as for the Savory crêpes, opposite.

Spread each warm crêpe with some of the chosen sweet filling, and then roll up. Sprinkle lightly with sugar, and serve.

SUGGESTED SWEET CRÊPE FILLINGS: The following recipes make ideal fillings for crêpes:

- Quince Cream (see page 20)
- Cotignac (see page 20)
- Damson Cheese (see page 25)
- Apricot Fool (see page 32)
- Hunza Jam (see page 32)
- Eighteenth-Century Apricot Ice Cream
(see page 33)
- Strawberries in Cream (see page 38)
- Strawberry Sauce (see page 38)
- Seventeeth-Century Raspberry Cream
(see page 40)
- Black Currant Jelly (see page 43)
- Gooseberry Fool (see page 47)
- Gooseberry and Mint Compote
(see page 47)

Classic Egg Desserts

There are so many ways of using eggs in desserts that it is difficult to be selective. Meringue baskets filled with fresh fruit make wonderful summer desserts, as do the many variations on the theme of custard-based puddings.

A Caramel Custard
This recipe is for good old-fashioned crème caramel.

SERVES 4

3 plus 4 tablespoons sugar

2 tablespoons water

2 cups milk

1 vanilla bean

2 eggs

Take an ordinary cake pan, and sprinkle in the 3 tablespoons of sugar over the bottom. Moisten with the water, and set on a heated burner over low heat until the sugar dissolves. Then turn the heat up, and boil briskly to a thick caramel color, tilting the pan around and around so the caramel cooks evenly. Remove from the heat, and let cool and set.

Simmer the milk with the vanilla bean for 5 minutes, then cool a little. Beat the eggs with the 4 tablespoons of sugar until thick, then pour on the warm milk, beating all the time. Pour onto the set caramel in the pan. Bake in a preheated oven at 300°F for 1–1½ hours, until it has set thoroughly. Cool completely in the pan before inverting onto a serving dish: The brown top will be glossy and the caramel sauce will run down the sides. Chill before serving.

Îles Flottantes
A very light dessert, "floating islands" are a masterpiece of French cuisine, and one of my favorite desserts. The pure white froth of the "islands," floating in a "sea" of pale yellow custard sauce, are as much a pleasure to the eye as they are to the palate.

SERVES 4

4 egg whites

a pinch of salt

½ cup sugar

2 recipe quantities *Crème Anglaise* (see page 153)

flaked almonds, toasted

Fill a shallow pan with water, and bring to simmering point. Beat the egg whites with a pinch of salt until they form stiff peaks. Whisk in the sugar gradually until the mixture becomes smooth and shiny. Spoon 4 tablespoon-sized heaps separately into the simmering water, and poach these "islands," turning once, for about 2–3 minutes, until risen and lightly set. Remove with a slotted spoon, and drain on a rack. Dry on absorbent paper towels, and place in a "lake" of *Crème Anglaise*. Chill thoroughly. Just before serving, sprinkle with the toasted almonds.

Queen of Puddings *This old-fashioned pudding is not just a useful way of using up eggs, it has become a classic for good reason. Wonderful for all seasons, it is sweet and comforting.*

SERVES 4

½ cup soft fresh bread crumbs

2 cups milk

2 tablespoons butter or margarine

grated rind of ½ lemon

3 eggs, separated

¾ cup sugar

3 tablespoons raspberry jam

candied cherries, to decorate

Grease a 3½ cup ovenproof dish, and sprinkle the bread crumbs over the bottom. Bring the milk to a slow simmer with the butter or margarine and all but 1 teaspoon of the lemon rind, then let cool. Beat the egg yolks with half the sugar. Strain the milk onto the beaten egg yolks, and stir until the mixture is quite smooth. Pour over the bread crumbs and let soak for 15 minutes.

Stand the dish in a pan of hot water, and bake in a preheated oven at 350°F for 25–30 minutes, until lightly set in the center. Cool a little on a wire rack. Warm the jam, and trickle it over the top of the pudding. Finally, beat the egg whites until very stiff, and gradually whisk in the remaining sugar. Beat until stiff and glossy. Fold in the remaining lemon rind, and pile the meringue on top of the pudding. Return to the oven, at the same temperature, for a further 20 minutes, until the meringue is crisp and lightly browned. Cool on a rack, decorate with candied cherries, and serve warm or cold.

In summer, serve this with a bowl of fresh raspberries. You could also use lemon curd in place of the raspberry jam.

Crème aux Fraises
For using up extra egg whites—for example, after making Mayonnaise (see page 122) or Crème Anglaise (see page 153)—this delicate dessert is beyond compare. Simplicity itself, it retains the freshness of ripe strawberries, is light in texture, and the most beautiful of summery pinks.

SERVES 4

1 lb strawberries, washed, dried, and hulled

2–3 tablespoons sugar

1 cup heavy cream, whipped

2 egg whites, stiffly beaten

Reserving four strawberries for garnish, purée the rest in a blender or food processor, and sweeten with the sugar. Stir into the whipped cream. Then carefully fold in the very stiffly beaten egg whites. Spoon into individual glass dishes, and chill. Decorate with the reserved strawberries, halved, just before serving.

Custard Tart
A light egg custard set inside a sweet pastry crust is traditional country fare. Made well, so that the custard is lightly set and not too sweet, it is delectable.

SERVES 4

1 recipe quantity Sweet Crust Dough (see page 150)

1 cup light cream or half-and-half

1 vanilla bean

strip of lemon peel

2 eggs and 1 egg yolk

6 tablespoons sugar

ground nutmeg

Roll out the dough, and use to line an 8-inch tart pan. Heat the cream or half-and-half in a heavy-bottomed saucepan with the vanilla bean and lemon peel, and bring slowly to simmering point. Let infuse for 10 minutes. Bring to a boil again, and remove from the heat. Cool. Beat the eggs, egg yolk, and sugar together until pale and thick. Strain the warm milk onto the egg mixture, stirring all the time, and then pour carefully into the prepared pastry shell. Sprinkle with ground nutmeg.

Bake in a preheated oven at 325°F for 30–40 minutes, until the top is firm to the touch. Remove from the heat, and cool on a wire rack. Eat when cold: Best eaten the same day.

Left: *Crème aux fraises*

field and *Countryside*

These hedgerows, hardly hedgerows,

little lines of sportive wood run wild.

William Wordsworth (1770–1850)

Food from the countryside has been aptly named "food for free." Scores of wild plants are, strictly speaking, edible, but here I am focusing on those which I regard as particularly delicious: Indeed, essential to my personal enjoyment of the seasons. Many of them are so prolific that there is no risk of their being obliterated: Nettles, blackberries, elder, and fat hen, for example, have survived picking for centuries, and many a gardener respects their persistence. Yet these "weeds," as we derogatively term them, have greater virtues. They have lovely tastes, and many are highly nutritious. The wild fruits of autumn fields are well known for their flavors, and some are even grown commercially because they are so popular.

One of the best things about cooking with wild plants is that it is fun. You go for a walk along a country road, basket in hand, and come back with a sense of pleasurable excitement in your "finds." What can match the feeling of the first days of spring, with their indescribable freshness, and a walk by fields, collecting young nettle tops for soup? Or blackberrying in a meadow in summer? Or picking apples in the first mists of fall, as the leaves begin to turn red-gold? This experience of the seasons is, in my opinion, considerably more delightful than a trip to the local supermarket.

Also, recipes with wild plants are part of an extremely ancient tradition. Throughout history man ate what was around him, and was far more familiar then we are today with the plants that had so much to offer him in his life. From eating what grew and lived around him, man moved on to farm and cultivate, losing sight of his original food source. It is only very recently that we in the West have bought our food with money, making us slaves to whatever is offered on the store shelf. Old cookbooks abound with recipes for wild plants, as naturally they do for fish or game. And not without good reason. Many people have heard of nettle soup simply because it is delicious. There is a hidden harvest out there which is ours for the picking: Judiciously, of course, and always with respect for Nature.

Remember, it is illegal to pick protected plants, and you should always pick your plants sparingly rather than denuding one area. Watch your step as you go, and don't trample delicate plants under your feet. Don't

pick from roadsides, since the plants will be contaminated by exhaust fumes, and do not trespass on private land. Do not touch or eat anything you are at all unsure of and wash all wild foods thoroughly. Observing these courtesies and precautions, we can enjoy the abundance of the countryside through its changing seasons, filling our baskets with natural produce which will reward us with its wonderful flavors.

A FEAST OF MUSHROOMS

From earliest times man has learned by trial and error the epicurean delights of wild mushrooms, and it is hard to match the excitement and pleasure of a trip into the woods and fields on a mushroom hunt. But even now, after centuries of study, there is still no theoretical way of distinguishing the edible from the poisonous: You can only tell by eating them, occasionally with fatal results. So man has cultivated a completely safe mushroom, *Agaricus bisporus*, which is what mushroom means to most of us: The one we buy in supermarkets.

But there are estimated to be over 2,000 species of edible fungi in the world (let alone inedible and invisible ones). There are certain mushrooms that are easily identifiable, and well worth taking home in your basket: Beefsteak polypores, blewits, boletes, chanterelles, fairy ring mushrooms, meadow mushrooms, honey mushrooms, morels, parasols, puffballs, oyster mushrooms, and inky caps. My best advice is that you join a mushroom club to learn how to identify your finds with more experienced collectors. Even so, it is prudent to accept an identification only if all the evidence confirms it. And if in doubt, don't eat them!

The mystery of the mushroom is that it is neither plant nor animal: It belongs to the world of microbes. By definition, mushrooms represent the group of fungi which form fruiting bodies visible to the naked eye, rather than microscopic ones. Toadstool is the traditional term for a poisonous fungus, but it is a vague and unsafe differentiation, since the margin between delicious mushroom and poisonous toadstool is narrow.

Mushrooms grow almost anywhere where there is dead organic matter: Compost, leaf litter, topsoil, straw, or dead wood. They are part of a vital ecological cycle in which plants produce, animals consume, and fungi reduce again. They play an essential part in the decomposition process, breaking down matter which can then be re-utilized. Mushrooms can be found almost all the year round.

Mushrooms are ephemeral: They appear, mature, and vanish in the space of a few days, perhaps weeks, and seldom appear twice in the same place. But if you keep your eyes open as you walk through fields and forests, you may discover some types of edible mushrooms.

Deep-Fried Mushrooms

Before people understood the nature of spore dispersal in mushrooms, they attributed fairy rings to fantastic phenomena: Either it was where lightning struck the ground, or it was snails moving around in perfect circles, or it was fairies catching colts grazing in the fields and riding around on their backs, or even the devil beating out a track during his nocturnal prowlings.

Dip each mushroom, or slice of mushroom, into the batter until coated all over.

small field mushrooms, or any edible wild mushrooms, wiped and sliced	**Fritter Batter (see page 154)** **oil for deep-frying**

Heat the oil to a very high temperature, then deep-fry the mushrooms for about 1 minute, turning until golden all over. Drain on absorbent paper towels, and serve immediately.

Try mushrooms dipped in spiced yogurt, or in soy sauce mixed with grated root ginger and a little garlic—both are tasty accompaniments.

Potted MUSHROOMS

When the moon is at the full,
Mushrooms you may freely pull;
But when the moon is on the wane,
Wait till you think to pluck again.

This old English saying may have been familiar to Eliza Acton when she wrote her cook book in 1845. Here is her way of preserving the rich harvest of mushrooms to eat throughout the lean days of winter. *Prepare either small flaps or buttons with great nicety, without wetting them, and wipe the former very dry, after the application of the salt and flannel. Stew them quite tender, with the same proportion of butter as the mushrooms au beurre [3 tablespoons to 2 cups], and salt, cayenne, and ground mace; when they are done turn them into a large dish, spread them over one end of it, and raise it two or three inches that they may be well drained from the butter. As soon as they are quite cold, press them very closely into small potting pans; pour lukewarm clarified butter thickly over them, and store them in a cool dry place. If intended for present use, merely turn them down upon a clean shelf; but for longer keeping cover the tops first with very dry paper, and then with melted mutton-suet. We have ourselves had the mushrooms, after being simply spread upon a dish while hot, remain perfectly good in that state for seven or eight weeks; they were prepared late in the season, and the weather was consequently cool during the interval.*

Mushrooms in Garlic Butter
In some parts of Europe there exists a tale which says that when St Peter was walking through a forest with Christ, eating bread that some villagers had given them, he spat some out on the ground and this turned into mushrooms. The devil, who was close behind, also spat on the ground and up sprang brightly colored, poisonous toadstools. Other sources claim that manna was mushrooms, which also seem to appear miraculously.

SERVES 3–4

1 lb wild mushrooms, such as puffballs, meadow
   mushrooms, cèpes, chanterelles, or boletes

¾ stick butter or margarine

2–3 garlic cloves, peeled and crushed

sea salt and freshly ground black pepper

chopped fresh parsley, to garnish

Clean and dry the mushrooms, and trim off any shaggy parts. Slice evenly.

Heat the butter or margarine in a large, heavy-bottomed pan, and toss the sliced mushrooms in it until they are well coated, and beginning to soften and cook through. Then add the crushed garlic, and cook for a further 1–2 minutes, tossing frequently. Remove from the heat, and season to taste with sea salt and pepper. Toss again, leave for several minutes in the pan, covered, for the juices to run, and then serve on hot plates, sprinkled with chopped fresh parsley.

Hops à l'Anvernoise
The French are very fond of hop tops—"jets d'houblon"—and make a wonderful soup with them. This simple way of cooking them as a side vegetable is exquisite, too: Well worth a try if you live where wild hops are plentiful. If not, asparagus tips make a good substitute in this recipe.

YOU WILL NEED: • hop tops , washed • Vegetable Stock (see page 154) • butter or margarine • cream • salt and freshly ground black pepper

Boil the hop tops—the top four leaves—in stock until tender, about 5–6 minutes. Drain, then toss over low heat with a little butter or margarine until well coated. Add a little cream to the pan, mix well, and season to taste. Serve immediately.

Comfrey Pie
Comfrey contains all the goodness of spinach, plus the valuable vitamin B12, which is otherwise not found in the vegetable world. It has a higher protein content than any other vegetable except soy beans, and has been eaten by man for over a thousand years. It is known in herbal medicine for its ability to help hasten the mending of fractured bones. Use spinach if comfrey is unavailable.

SERVES 4

1 recipe quantity Oil Dough (see page 152)

2 cups comfrey, washed, drained, chopped, and
  lightly cooked

2 garlic cloves, peeled and crushed

1 recipe quantity Béchamel Sauce (see page 154)

salt and freshly ground black pepper

2 tablespoons heavy cream

2 eggs, separated

Press the dough, with your knuckles, into a greased 9 in pie dish. Bake blind (see page 152) in a preheated oven at 325°F for 10–15 minutes, until set and lightly golden.

Mix the comfrey and crushed garlic into the Béchamel Sauce, season to taste, and add the cream. Add the egg yolks to the mixture. Beat the whites until stiff, and fold them in. Pour into the pastry shell, and bake in a preheated oven at 375°F for 25–30 minutes, until risen, golden, and lightly set in the center.

Dandelion SALADS

Dandelion gets its name from *dent de lion*, meaning lion's tooth, and describing its jagged leaves. Dandelion wine, made from the flowers, is a well-known country wine, but the leaves have also been used in salads for centuries. They still are in France today, tossed into mixed leaf salads and appreciated for their bitter flavor and richness of vitamins.

• Potato Salad with Dandelion: Cook waxy new potatoes, and slice them while still hot. Chop a few scallions, crush a clove of garlic, slice some inner celery stalks very finely, and tear up some young dandelion leaves. Toss them all together with the potatoes in Vinaigrette (see page 155).

• Similarly, Beet and Dandelion Salad with young freshly cooked, chopped beets is delicious.

• Or try an Egg and Dandelion Salad: Boil the eggs until the yolks are soft but not runny. Peel, quarter, and place on a bed of washed, shredded dandelion leaves, dressed in Vinaigrette (see page 155).

• Equally good is Dandelion and Pasta Salad: Just tear the young dandelion leaves into little strips, and toss with cold, cooked pasta in lots of garlicky Vinaigrette (see page 155). Add small cubes of cooked zucchini, and toss again.

Nettle Soup
In Europe, young nettles are a traditional Spring tonic, made in the form of soup or tea. For country folk they were the first green vegetable to appear after a long, lean winter's diet of salted meat. They are rich in vegetable protein, minerals, and vitamins, and were said to purify the blood. This recipe is equally delicious made with cooked spinach.

SERVES 4

a large saucepan full of nettle tops

3 tablespoons butter or margarine

¼ cup flour

3 cups Vegetable Stock (see page 154)

salt and freshly ground black pepper

½ cup light cream or half-and-half

Croûtons (see page 155), to serve

Wash the nettle tops, and drain well. Cook in just the water still clinging to them, as for spinach, covered, for 10–15 minutes, until completely tender. This will neutralise the sting and release a dark colored water. Drain well, and chop the nettles.

Melt the butter or margarine, and stir in the flour. Add the stock gradually, stirring all the time, until the mixture is smooth and thick. Simmer very gently for 5 minutes, then season to taste. Mix in the cooked nettles, and then purée in a blender or food processor. Add the cream or half-and-half, reheat gently, and it is ready to serve. Pour into large, shallow soup dishes, and sprinkle the Croûtons over the top.

Fat Hen au Gratin
Fat hen was a common vegetable for country folk from neolithic times, superseded only when spinach—its close relative—began to be cultivated in earnest. It is a sensational vegetable, rich in B vitamins, high in vegetable protein, and has more iron and calcium than spinach. Purple sprouting broccoli or broccoli rabe may be used as a substitute.

SERVES 4

1½ lb fat hen, trimmed and washed

butter or margarine

salt and freshly ground black pepper

4 soft-boiled eggs, cooled, peeled, and halved

1½ recipe quantities Béchamel Sauce (see page 154)

a little light cream

½ cup fine dry bread crumbs, fried in vegetable oil

Put the prepared fat hen into a large saucepan with a little water, and boil until tender, about 8 minutes. Drain and chop it, then toss in butter or margarine over low heat, and season to taste. Cover the bottom of an oven-proof dish with the fat hen, then place the halved eggs on top. (The yolks should be soft but not runny.) Pour the Béchamel Sauce over the top, dot with more butter or margarine, and bake in a preheated oven at 400°F for 20 minutes, until the top is golden. Sprinkle with the fried bread crumbs, and serve.

Walnut Bread
The magnificent walnut tree makes a strong statement in the landscape, with its stately growth, its large, smooth leaves, and its enormous span. Its fruits, the wonderful "wet" walnuts of the fall, are at their best fresh. You can make soup with them, and put them into nut roasts, salads, or leek dishes. This bread is also a superb way of enjoying their flavor.

MAKES 2 X 1 LB LOAVES

2 eggs

½ cup light brown sugar

4 cups all-purpose flour

½ teaspoon salt

4 teaspoons baking powder

2 cups milk

1½ cups chopped walnuts

Beat the eggs well, and then beat in the brown sugar. Sift the flour with the salt and baking powder, and add alternately with the milk to the egg mixture. Stir in the chopped nuts, and pour into two greased 1 lb loaf pans. Let stand, covered, in a warm place for 30 minutes. Then bake at 350°F for 45 minutes. Cool a little on a wire rack, and then slice and serve.

Blueberry or Bilberry cake
If you are lucky enough to live where bilberries grow plentifully in the wild, they are a rewarding harvest. They make an excellent country wine, and a delicious pie, traditionally served in England for Sunday lunch with lots of heavy cream! This cake, which you can also make with cultivated blueberries, is succulent, moist, and very more-ish. It freezes well, too, so you can enjoy it through the dark days of winter.

SERVES 8

2¼ cups self-rising flour

2 teaspoons ground cinnamon

2½ sticks margarine

½ cup sugar

grated rind of ½ lemon

¾ lb blueberries or bilberries

2 eggs, beaten

Sift the flour with the cinnamon, and then rub in the margarine until the mixture resembles crumbs. Stir in the sugar and lemon rind, and then fold in the berries carefully. Fold in the beaten eggs gently, and put into a greased 8-inch cake pan with a removable bottom. Bake in a preheated oven at 350°F for 1¼ hours, until a knife comes out clean from the center. Leave in the pan for about 10 minutes, then remove and place on a wire rack to cool.

Verjuice

VERJUICE OF CRAB APPLES : *"Gather crabbs as soon as the kernels turn black, and lay they in a heap to sweat and take them into troughs and crush with beetles [heavy wooden mallet]. Make a bagge of coarse hair-cloth and fill it with the crabbes, and presse and run the liquor into Hogsheads."*

Food in England, Dorothy Hartley, 1954

Verjuice was in constant use until the nineteenth century, when its place was taken by the squeeze of lemon juice. It is really a very sharp cider, not a vinegar. The distilling was of interest, for it would account for the apparent mildness of some of the pickles made. In copying old recipes, very often hard cider is much nearer the original than modern vinegar.

Crab Apple Jelly *Was the crab apple the tree whose fruit tempted Eve in the Garden of Eden? We may never know, but in any case the crab apple has been eaten by man since the dawn of history, and is a versatile and useful fruit. It makes the best of all the hedgerow jellies, a beautiful orange-pink color, with an individual flavor. It is delicious with hot or cold meats, with bread and cheese, or on toast.*

YOU WILL NEED: • crab apples • water • granulated sugar

Cook the crab apples with water to cover until they are very soft. Strain through a jelly bag, and let drip for several hours. Measure the liquid collected into a clean pan, and to every 2 cups liquid add 1½ cups sugar. Dissolve the sugar over gentle heat, and then boil rapidly to setting point (see page 145). Cool a little, then can and seal (see page 145). Store in a cool, dark place.

You can make composite hedgerow jellies *ad infinitum.* Try crab apple and blackberry, crab apple and rowanberry, crab apple and rosehip, or crab apple and elderberry. You can also add the leaf of a scented geranium to the cooking of the final jelly to add a delicate flavor. Remove it before potting the jelly.

Blackberry PURÉE

This makes a delicious fruity sauce to serve with the pudding or dessert of your choice, and is a good base for Blackberry Ice Cream (see page 140).

Put 1 lb blackberries, washed and hulled, into a blender or food processor with a little sugar, and blend to a purée. Press through a strainer to remove the seeds, and sweeten to taste with more sugar. This amount will make approximately 2 cups, according to the juiciness of the fruit.

Pickled Blackberries

The greatest taste of the hedgerow harvest, blackberries have been eaten for centuries. Other parts of the plant have been fully used too: The pliable twigs for basket work, and the leaves and roots for natural dyes. Pickling blackberries is an excellent way of preserving them, and they are wonderful with a simple lunch of bread and cheese and salad.

MAKES 4 LB

1 lb sugar

½ cup white vinegar

1 teaspoon allspice berries

1 teaspoon whole cloves

2 x 3-inch cinnamon sticks

2 lb blackberries, washed and hulled

Dissolve the sugar in the vinegar over gentle heat. Put the spices in a cheesecloth bag, add to the vinegar, and simmer for several minutes. Add the blackberries, and cook for 10–15 minutes. Remove the bag of spices, scoop out the blackberries with a slotted spoon, and pack into warm, sterilized jars. Then boil the vinegar down until it turns syrupy. Pour over the blackberries in the jars to cover, and seal (see page 145). Store in a cool, dark place.

Blackberry Ice Cream

This is nothing less than sublime, making the very best use of a superlative fall hedgerow fruit. You will enjoy this as the winter days darken and evenings close in.

SERVES 4

½ cup plain yogurt

½ cup *Crème Anglaise* (see page 153)

⅓ cup confectioners' sugar

½ recipe quantity Blackberry Purée (see page 139)

2 egg whites

a pinch of salt

Mix the yogurt with the *Crème Anglaise*, and sweeten with the sugar. Beat well until smooth. Fold in the Blackberry Purée. Beat the egg whites with a pinch of salt until they are very stiff, and fold into the mixture. Put into a freezer container, cover, and freeze for 1 hour, until firmish at the edge. Scoop out, and blend until smooth. Return to the container, cover, and return to the freezer for the final freezing. Alternatively, use an ice-cream maker, following the manufacturer's instructions.

Right: *Pickled blackberries*

simple *Preserves*

Now it is autumn and the falling fruit

And the long journey towards oblivion

D. H. Lawrence (1885–1930)

When the garden harvest provides a glut of fruits and vegetables, one of the best ways of utilizing them, apart from freezing made-up dishes, is to make preserves. Jams, jellies, chutneys, relishes, and conserves are traditional ways of stocking the larder; there are many books devoted to the skills of good preserve-making.

Jams and Jellies

Use fruit which is firm and ripe, or just under-ripe, and of good quality. Over-ripe fruit will not produce jam which sets well. In a wet season, fruit has a lower sugar content than normal, so jam or jelly made from it may not keep well for as long. Always wash fruit before using, to remove all traces of dust and dirt. Use cube, preserving, or granulated sugar—in that order of preference—and avoid dark sugars since they change both the color and flavor of the preserve. If you warm the sugar slightly before stirring into the fruit, it will dissolve more quickly.

CRYSTALLIZING AND PECTIN

If your jam should crystallize during storage it is due either to too much sugar, or to over-boiling. It also happens if the storage place is too dry. You can produce a short-term remedy by pouring the contents of the jar into a saucepan and heating gently to near boiling point. Let reset in a clean jar. The jam will be satisfactory for immediate use, although it will go sugary again in time.

Pectin is a natural gum-like substance found in varying amounts in different fruits—usually in cores, seeds, and peel—and is essential for a good set in jams and jellies. Some fruits do not contain enough pectin for a good set, so you need to mix low- with high-pectin fruits, or add pectin in liquid or powder form.

Guide to PECTIN CONTENTS OF FRUIT

HIGH	MEDIUM	LOW
tart apples	sweet apples	late blackberries
black currants	fresh apricots	cherries
cranberries	early blackberries	elderberries
damsons	greengages	figs
gooseberries	peaches	guavas
grapefruit	plums	medlars
grapes	raspberries	mulberries
lemons		pears
loganberries		rhubarb
acidic plums		strawberries
quinces		English marrow
red currants		

EQUIPMENT

Preserving Pan: Choose a pan which will be large enough: It should not be more than half-full when the fruit and sugar are added, because the mixture needs to be able to boil rapidly without boiling over. Choose a heavy-bottomed aluminum or stainless-steel pan for best results. Never use an iron or zinc pan, because the acid in the fruit reacts with the metal, and both the color and flavor of the preserve will be affected. Enamel pans do not conduct heat fast enough, and tend to burn easily. Using a copper pan destroys much of the vitamin C content of the fruit.

OTHER EQUIPMENT

- large hair or nylon strainer (metal equipment will impair the flavor of the preserve, and can be discolored by the acid in the fruit)
- slotted spoon
- long-handled wooden spoons
- sharp stainless-steel knives
- mincer or food processor
- serrated knife
- pitter, for pitting small fruit
- funnel
- accurate scales
- jars with plastic screw-tops (metal ones rust) or glass tops
- jam thermometer
- waxed and plastic discs
- labels

Making Jam

A jam is a conserve of fruit, boiled with sugar and water, whereas a jelly is made with the fruit juice only, boiled with sugar. A marmalade is a kind of jam made with citrus fruits. Jams must have sufficient sugar for sound storage: Organisms cannot grow when the sugar content is more than 50–55 per cent. Hence the addition of lemon juice in many jam recipes—its twofold purpose being to relieve the sweetness and also to help the set. Jams are usually cooked to 220°F. Remember that it is the fruit rather than the sugar that needs cooking, so jams (and jellies) boiled for too long with the sugar tend to lose color and flavor. Certain soft fruits can be ruined by long boiling.

BASIC METHOD

Place washed fruit in preserving pan, with or without water as per the recipe. Cook gently, without boiling, until juices begin to run. Turn up heat, bring to boil, then simmer until tender. Add the sugar, and stir over gentle heat until it dissolves. Bring to a boil, boil rapidly to setting point (see below). Can, cover, and store (see below).

TESTING FOR A SET

Flake test: When the jam starts to thicken, dip in a wooden spoon and hold it over the pan. If, as the jam drops off the spoon, it forms a sheet and drops off as cleanly as a flake, then the jam will set when cold. If by any chance the jam fails to set, add 2 tablespoons lemon juice per 4 lb fruit, and try again—or add pectin in the quantity suggested on the label.

Saucer test: When it starts to thicken, put a little jam on a cold saucer; put in a cold place. Draw jam off the heat. After 5 minutes, tilt the saucer: If the jam wrinkles a little and doesn't run, it is ready to can. If it's still liquid and runs over the saucer, return jam to the heat. Continue boiling until the test is successful. The stage of boiling the sugar to setting point generally takes about 10 minutes, but depends on the water content of the fruit.

Thermometer: You will need a reliable cook's thermometer, which goes up to and includes 220°F. Always put the thermometer into hot water before use to prevent it cracking. To test for a set, stir the jam so that the temperature is even throughout, and when the thermometer reads 220°F, a good set should be obtained, although in some cases 221–222°F will be better.

CANNING, COVERING AND STORAGE

Let jam settle before potting, and remove any scum. Choose suitably sized jam jars with plastic or glass lids. Sterilize in boiling water or a dishwasher, dry, and keep warm in a very low oven until ready to use. Fill the jars up to the neck. Cover immediately with a waxed paper circle, waxed side down. Let cool, then place a piece of plastic wrap over the top of each jar, and put the lid on over it. Try to avoid metal screw-tops, as they tend to corrode. Label clearly (date and contents) and store in a cool, dark, dry place.

Making Jellies *So long as you have the basic equipment of a jelly bag and a thermometer, making jellies is simpler than making any other preserve. Always make sure that the jelly bag is clean, by soaking it in boiling water, then wringing it out.*

The most practical way of hanging a jelly bag is on the legs of an upturned chair. Tie the suspending tapes to the bars of the chair, and place a large bowl underneath to catch the drips. Never squeeze the bag to extract more juice because the jelly will turn cloudy.

BASIC METHOD

Make sure that the fruit you are using is clean and not over-ripe. Remove any stems, but don't bother to clean fruits such as gooseberries and black currants. Pick the fruit over and discard any that is moldy or over-ripe. If you are gathering the fruit from the hedgerow or your own garden, it is best to pick on a dry day because fruit sodden with rain will attract mildew. Rinse the fruit to remove any dirt or grit.

Put the fruit in a preserving pan, and cook as instructed in the recipe until the fruit is soft and the juices run. Strain through the scalded jelly bag (see above), and measure the juice collected into the cleaned pan. Add the sugar: The general rule for jelly is to add 2 cups of sugar to every 2 cups of juice. This gives jelly which will both set and keep, although this ratio varies slightly according to the fruit.

Stir over medium heat until the sugar dissolves, then bring to a boil and boil fast to setting point (the same as for jam—see page 145). This will take about 10 minutes, longer if the fruit has a high water content.

Skim the jelly with a metal spoon and remove the last traces of scum with a piece of absorbent paper towel. Can immediately in warm, sterilized jars (see page 145), before it has a chance to set in the pan. Cover, and store (see page 145).

Suitable Fruits for JELLY MAKING

windfall apples	haws	raspberries
blackberries	japonica	red currants
black currants	loganberries	rosehips
cherries	medlars	rowan
crab apples	mulberries	sloes
damsons or wild plums	pears	strawberries
elderberries	plums	white currants
gooseberries	quinces	

Chutneys A wide variety of fruits and vegetables can be used to make

chutney. Traditionally, apples and onions provided the basis, and golden raisins, raisins, and

dates are often found in the ingredients list, too. Plums, English marrows, gooseberries, and

tomatoes also make lovely chutney, and shallots and garlic are often added to give zest and

flavor. Chutneys are frequently laced with hot spices such as chilies, peppercorns, and mustard

seeds to provide a hot tang.

Making Chutney *Use fresh fruit or vegetables which are not over-ripe or damaged. Prepare*

them, and put into an aluminum pan (metals such as brass, copper, or iron will react with the acid in the vinegar and
spoil both the chutney and the pan). Usually, unless otherwise specified in the recipe, all the other ingredients—the onions,
spices, vinegar, and sugar, etc.—are put in the pan together with the vegetables or fruit. They are simmered for 2–3 hours,
according to the individual recipe. This long, steady cooking is required for a good chutney, but do not over-boil it. As
soon as the mixture thickens to the point where pools of vinegar no longer collect on the surface, the chutney is ready.

Allow the cooked chutney to cool for a while in the preserving pan before bottling because it tends to shrink quite
considerably as it loses heat. Can in sterilized jars when tepid, prodding out any air bubbles trapped in the mixture, and
making sure that the chutney is well packed down. (See page 145 for canning and storing.) Some chutneys keep for many
years, and improve greatly with keeping.

Pickled Vegetables and
Relishes You can use a wide range of fruits, vegetables, and herbs for

making pickled vegetables and relishes: Cauliflower, shallots, apples, onions, artichokes, beets,

peaches, and pears, for example. Baby cucumbers and red cabbage are delicious pickled, as are

mushrooms and even walnuts. The art of making good pickles is to get the right balance of sour-

ness, saltiness, and sweetness by adjusting the quantities of vinegar, salt, and sugar.

Brining

Vegetables and fruits are often soaked in brine, a solution of salt and water, to help preserve them, prior to pickling in vinegar. A 10 per cent brine solution is normally used for most vegetable pickles and relishes. Sometimes vinegar is used with the brine, and then the percentage can be lowered to 5 per cent.

TO MAKE BRINE: For a 10 per cent brine solution, mix ½ cup salt to every 4 cups water. Stir until the salt dissolves.

For a 5 per cent brine solution, mix ¼ cup salt to every 4 cups water.

BASIC METHOD FOR PICKLING

Clean and prepare the vegetables or fruit, cut up to a suitable size, and cover with a 10 per cent brine solution (see above) for 24 hours. Keep weighted down with a plate, so that the vegetables or fruit remain completely covered.

Drain, rinse thoroughly with cold water, and pack into jars. Pour Spiced Vinegar (see below) over them. Cover, and seal.

Crisp pickles, such as onions and red cabbage, are best covered with cold vinegar, whereas plums, damsons, and walnuts are better covered with boiling or very hot vinegar, which is allowed to cool before covering and sealing.

SPICES AND HERBS: Spices add zest and flavor to pickled vegetables and relishes, and also have the added advantage that they are preservatives in their own right. The best ones to use are cloves, cinnamon, pepper, allspice, mace, nutmeg, and ginger. Ground turmeric is sometimes added for its golden color. Herbs are a traditional addition to many relishes and pickles, notably rue, fennel, sage, cilantro—and, of course, dill.

Spiced Vinegar

MAKES 4 CUPS:

4 cups white vinegar

1-inch cube root ginger

¼ cup whole cloves, allspice berries, cinnamon sticks, and whole black peppercorns

Warm the vinegar in an aluminum preserving pan. Add the spices, cover, and infuse over low heat for 2 hours. Let cool. When completely cold, strain and decant into bottles with the spices. Use as required.

basic *Recipes*

Shortcake Dough

FOR AN 8–10 IN PIE SHELL

2 cups all-purpose flour

a pinch of salt

1 stick butter or margarine, cut into small pieces

Sift the flour with the salt into a large bowl. Rub in the butter or margarine until the mixture resembles fine bread crumbs. Add a little cold water, enough to mix to a light dough. Knead on a floured surface until smooth. Chill for 30 minutes before using.

Sweet Crust Dough

Rub the butter or sunflower margarine into the sifted flour until it resembles fine bread crumbs, then mix in

FOR AN 8–10 IN PIE SHELL

¾ stick butter or sunflower margarine, cut into small
  pieces

1½ cups all-purpose flour, sifted

1 heaping tablespoon sugar

3–4 tablespoons very cold water

the sugar. Add the cold water, and knead the dough on a floured surface until light and smooth. Chill for 2 hours before rolling out.

This dough freezes very successfully.

Oil Dough

FOR AN 8–9 INCH PIE SHELL

1½ cups all-purpose flour

½ teaspoon salt

1 tablespoon sesame seeds (optional)

5 tablespoons vegetable oil

1½ tablespoons cold water

Sift the flour with the salt into a large bowl, and stir in the sesame seeds, if using, oil, and water. Mix well, then knead briefly until smooth. Press immediately into a greased tart pan or pie dish with your knuckles. This dough does not need chilling before use.

Blender Dough

FOR AN 8–9 IN PIE SHELL

6 tablespoons soft margarine

1½ cups all-purpose flour

3 tablespoons cold water

a large pinch salt

Put all the ingredients into a blender or food processor, and blend until they form a dough. Knead to a smooth ball, and chill for 1 hour before using.

To Bake Blind

Line the greased pie dish or tart pan with the prepared dough. Cut out a piece of aluminum foil or wax paper larger than the bottom of the dish or pan, and press it against the dough. Then fill the pie shell with a ½-inch layer of dried beans or ceramic baking beans. For a partially baked pie shell, bake in a preheated oven at 350°F for 10–15 minutes, then remove the aluminum foil or paper and beans, and bake for a further 5 minutes, until just firm and lightly colored. Pie shells which need complete baking should be returned to the oven for 15 minutes after removing the foil and beans, until firm and pale golden brown. Time and temperature may vary from recipe to recipe.

Crème Anglaise

MAKES ABOUT 2 CUPS

6 tablespoons sugar

2 egg yolks or 1 whole egg

1 heaped teaspoon cornstarch

1½ cups hot milk

1 teaspoon vanilla extract

Beat the sugar with the egg yolks or whole egg (the latter makes a lighter custard sauce) until thick and creamy. The mixture will turn pale yellow. Beat in the cornstarch. Continue beating while you pour on the hot milk in a thin stream, until the mixture is well blended. Pour into a heavy-bottomed saucepan and cook gently over moderate heat, stirring all the time with a wooden spoon. When it begins to thicken and turn creamy, turn the heat down, allow it to come to a very gentle simmer, and continue stirring for 1–2 minutes. Do not let it boil hard, otherwise it will separate. Remove from the heat and stir in the vanilla extract. Let settle for 5–10 minutes before serving. *Crème Anglaise* can also be served cold.

Frangipani *Frangipani is an almond-flavored* crème pâtissière *(see below), the "pastry cream" basis of many a classic French dessert.*

1 egg

1 egg yolk

6 tablespoons sugar

½ cup sifted all-purpose flour

1 cup boiling milk

3 tablespoons butter

2 teaspoons vanilla extract

1 teaspoon almond extract

1½ cups crushed macaroons or ground almonds,

  or half and half

Beat the whole egg and egg yolk together, and gradually add the sugar, beating until the mixture is pale yellow and thick. Beat in the flour, then whisk in the hot milk in a thin stream. Pour into a heavy-bottomed saucepan, and place over moderate heat. Stir slowly as it thickens, and when it bubbles turn the heat down and stir for a further 2–3 minutes.

    Beat in the butter, vanilla and almond extracts, and the macaroons or almonds. Cool, and use.

Crème Pâtissière

To make, simply follow the Frangipani recipe above, omitting the almond extract and crushed macaroons or ground almonds; just flavor it with vanilla extract.

Fritter Batter

MAKES ABOUT 1 CUP

1 cup all-purpose flour

a pinch of salt

1 teaspoon baking powder

2 tablespoons olive oil

½ cup warm water

1 egg white, stiffly beaten

Sift the flour with the salt and baking powder, and stir in the oil. Gradually add the water and stir well until the mixture is thick and creamy. Let stand for 2 hours, and then thin out with a little more water if necessary. Fold the stiffly beaten egg white into the mixture just before using it.

Vegetable Stock

If you decide not to use store-bought bouillon cubes, you can easily make your own vegetable stock from vegetable trimmings.

Using the trimmings from vegetables such as onions, carrots, leeks, cabbage, tomatoes, Jerusalem artichokes, potatoes (including the peelings), cauliflower (including leaves), and so on, makes the most of them.

Simply put the trimmings into a large saucepan, and cover with cold water. Add sea salt, peppercorns, and bay leaves or other herbs for flavoring, either fresh or dried and according to taste. Bring to a boil, then simmer, covered, for 1 hour. Let stand until cold, then strain off.

This stock will keep in the refrigerator for up to 5 days. Alternatively, it freezes very well.

Béchamel Sauce

MAKES ABOUT 2 CUPS

3 tablespoons butter or margarine

2 tablespoons flour

1 cup warmed milk

Melt the butter or margarine in a thick-bottomed pan, and stir in the flour with a wooden spoon. Add the milk slowly, stirring all the time, until the sauce thickens. Season to taste, and simmer over very gentle heat for 6–8 minutes. Thin out with more milk if necessary.

FOR SAUCE À LA CRÈME: Make the sauce with light cream instead of milk.

Vinaigrette

MAKES ABOUT 1 CUP

2 teaspoons Dijon mustard

2 tablespoons lemon juice or wine vinegar

sea salt and freshly ground black pepper

½ teaspoon sugar (optional)

1 garlic clove, peeled and crushed (optional)

½ cup olive oil

fresh rosemary or bay leaf (optional)

Mix the Dijon mustard with the lemon juice or wine vinegar, and season with sea salt and pepper. Add the sugar and crushed garlic, if desired. Add the olive oil gradually, stirring thoroughly all the time, until the mixture thickens and amalgamates. Let stand for a while before using, so that the flavors blend well. Put a few rosemary leaves or a small bay leaf into the vinaigrette if you wish, and it will take on the subtle flavor of the herb.

Melba Toast

Cut the crusts off very thin slices of wholewheat or white bread, according to taste. Lay them in a single layer on a baking tray, and put into a preheated oven set at 300°F. Leave until crisp and lightly browned, about 40 minutes.

Croûtons

SERVES 4

4 slices white or wholewheat bread, medium thick,
  crusts removed

sunflower or peanut oil for frying

Cut the slices of bread into tiny cubes. Heat the oil gently, and sauté the cubes of bread over medium heat, shaking regularly to turn them, until they begin to crisp and eventually turn a light golden color. Remove the croûtons from the pan with a slotted spoon, and drain on absorbent kitchen paper. Keep in a warm oven until ready to use—an ideal accompaniment to soups and salads.

menu index

index

Figures in italics refer to illustration captions.

First published in the United States of America in 1998
by Abbeville Press,
488 Madison Avenue, New York, N.Y. 10022

First published in Great Britain in 1997 by
George Weidenfeld & Nicolson Limited

First edition
2 4 6 8 10 9 7 5 3 1

WARNING: The Publishers assume no responsibility for any ill effects or illness
caused by the gathering or consumption of any wild plants. It is imperative to learn how
to identify wild plants before you begin eating them. Until you are an experienced col-
lector, do not eat wild plants unless an expert verifies that they are edible.

Printed and bound in Italy.

ISBN 0-7892-0419-3

Designed by Lisa Tai
Home Economist: Emma Patmore
Stylist: Roisin Nield